"Want to know how to motivate your people? Read *Everyday People, Extraordinary Leadership*. It will demonstrate that getting people to follow your lead is not like throwing a switch. You need to reach their hearts and their minds. Words are important, but more important are your actions. Jim Kouzes and Barry Posner are two of the best thinkers (and doers) in the leadership arena. Seldom have I walked into the office without seeing a copy of one of their leadership books. The young women and men who first read Jim and Barry's books are now leading their organizations. So, it is fitting that *Everyday People, Extraordinary Leadership* comes out now. Our times are challenging and leadership is more important than ever. Read this book and come away with ideas that will invigorate your leadership and inspire others to follow your lead."
—**John Baldoni,** member of Marshall Goldsmith 100 Coaches, Global Guru
Top 30 Leadership expert, and author of 14 books, including his newest
GRACE: A Leader's Guide to a Better Us

"Uplifting, insightful, practical, and powerful! The stories and examples packed into this book clarify what leadership means, why it matters, and how everyone can (and should!) lead. Thank you, Jim and Barry, for this valuable gem!"
—**Deb Calvert,** president of People First Productivity Solutions, coauthor,
Stop Selling and Start Leading

"In my first foray into *The Leadership Challenge* world of Jim Kouzes and Barry Posner, I was presented with the idea that "The road to the future is unpaved." This latest addition to their incredible literary toolbox provides the reader with a clear path to that future, one that clearly defines both the scenic route and potential roadblocks. It is current, timely, and instructive, and emphasizes above all that leadership truly is everyone's business."
—**Alan Lyme,** LISW, Certified Master for The Leadership Challenge, MINT
Certified MI Trainer

"The world needs strong leadership today more than ever before and Jim Kouzes and Barry Posner show us the difference extraordinary leaders are making with their teams, organizations, and communities. In their newest book, *Everyday People, Extraordinary Leadership*, Jim and Barry do a masterful job of providing us with wonderful leadership stories and lessons learned from everyday people centered around The Five Practices of Exemplary Leadership. This is a must-read book for any leader who is looking to make a positive impact with those they serve."
—**Brent Kondritz,** Executive Director, Center for Leadership,
University of Dayton

"Local communities are facing unique challenges: social unrest, catastrophic weather events, and a need for truth and understanding. As a local news organization, Scripps has challenged ourselves to create an authentic connection with our viewers through essential journalism and meaningful storytelling. *The Leadership Challenge* provided the framework for our company to hold the discussions that help us manage change. Now, Jim Kouzes and Barry Posner take that to the next level, recognizing there are leaders at all levels and no one needs a title to be a leader."
—**Brian Lawlor,** President, Local Media, The E.W. Scripps Company

"At a time when impact and influence is needed most, Jim Kouzes and Barry Posner provide us with a roadmap for each of us to be our very best. I am thrilled about this latest book, *Everyday People, Extraordinary Leadership*. We know leadership is NOT a title; it's all about behavior influencing and empowering others. In my business, the true 1:1 leadership occurs between every nurse and patient wherever care is delivered. Jim and Barry teach us from over 30 years of research a practical yet profound way to get up every day, show up every day, wherever that is, to make a difference in this world through our words, actions, and behaviors toward those around us."
—**Lori Armstrong,** CEO & Chief Clinical Officer, Inspire Nurse Leaders, and Adjunct Professor, Drexel University

"Jim Kouzes and Barry Posner have consistently helped millions of people across the globe every day as they grow and lead. Their latest book, *Everyday People, Exemplary Leadership* takes their seminal work to the next level, providing data based, yet very practical guidance based on their decades of experience and research. Whether you are just starting your career, or are a seasoned exec, you will learn the core tenets of exemplary leadership that really do apply to everybody! Read this book—you will grow."
—**Ann Herrmann-Nehdi,** Chair of the Board, Herrmann Inc.

"Now more than ever (a phrase we're hearing a lot these days), leadership is important. And while that's true, the reality is that it's always been true. Kouzes and Posner's wonderful new book illuminates a subject that is both timeless and timely. Its principles are not defined by a particular era; yet, they are

hyper-relevant to today's unique challenges and crises. This is a book for leaders. And guess what? That includes you, because whether you know it or not, and regardless of your position or title, you are already leading. This book will help you to do it with conscious intent, and, therefore, to do it better. And that's exactly what we all need—now more than ever."
—**Steve Farber,** Founder, The Extreme Leadership Institute, author, *The Radical Leap, Greater Than Yourself,* and *Love Is Just Damn Good Business*

"Jim Kouzes and Barry Posner have done it again! Their new book *Everyday People, Extraordinary Leadership* expands on the excellent foundation of their earlier book, *The Five Practices of Exemplary Leadership.* They bring not only empirical research but also real life examples of leadership qualities and practices that everyday people use to make the extraordinary happen."
—**Louise Aryapour,** CFO, Catholic Charities of Santa Clara County

"Growing up in the late 1960's and 70's, I was driven to read all I could about leadership, set goals, observe others, and make lists of traits that good leaders displayed. I read many, many books to learn those action steps. I would challenge myself, engage others for support, and practice deliberately. My obsession with continuous learning and training made all the difference. I wish I would have had this book back then. This book really simplifies the process, which took me over 10 years to finally feel confident in my ability to lead. I could have had that 'roadmap' in just one book. I congratulate James and Barry on another great leadership book."
—**Dwight Conover,** Chairman, Northwest Financial Corporation

"Kouzes and Posner have done it again! Reminding us that no matter our role, *everyone* has the capacity for significant leadership impact in their lives, workplaces, and communities. Their research confirms that it is not personality or charisma that produces leaders, but a specific set of measurable and replicable behaviors. And then they provide exercises we can *all* undertake to strengthen those very same competencies. A practical and inspiring guidebook to leadership for all!"
—**Darrell Evora,** CEO, Uplift Family Services

"*Everyday People, Extraordinary Leadership* perfectly illustrates Jim Kouzes and Barry Posner's idea that "leadership is everyone's business. It is a simple, yet profound leadership model for everyone regardless of your title, position, or authority.

To demonstrate this point, let me show you the difference between the old train (what we called green train) in the past and the bullet train which runs throughout China now. The old train has one engine in the front of the train and it drags all the cars. That's why the speed is very slow.

However, with the bullet train, each car has its own engine and the cars work together collectively. Thus, the bullet train is super fast. As a parallel to organizational leadership, if it is only one leader that takes the leading role, it is harder for him or her to lead. However, if everyone is ignited, enabled, and empowered, the ordinary people can make the extraordinary difference, they can start their own engines, and take personal responsibilities. The impact will be huge—everyone will feel responsible and engaged, team morale will be boosted, and the company's financial performance will improve.

With the deliberate practice according to the leadership model, anyone can become an extraordinary leader and make the difference anytime and anywhere they want.
—**Connie Stevens**, Founder, HeadStart Consulting Company (Shanghai)

"With *Everyday People, Extraordinary Leadership*, Barry Posner and James Kouzes have presented a new vision of leadership. Not limited to the nominal leaders or specific groups of managers but for all of us. The book guides us through five practices of leadership everyone can learn and use at work, school, or everyday life. All practices are proven by carefully collected data and memorable examples.

For me as someone who mainly works with virtual teams and who has to lead people who are not directly reporting to me or even are on a higher manage-ment level, the five practices of extraordinary leadership provide easy-to-apply methods for successful collaboration with my team members. Thank you."
—**Alex Schiller**, Senior Global Account Manager Automotive, Micron Technology

Everyday People,

Extraordinary Leadership

JAMES M. KOUZES
BARRY Z. POSNER

Everyday People,

Extraordinary Leadership

How to
Make a Difference
Regardless of Your
Title, Role, or Authority

The**Leadership**
Challenge®
A Wiley Brand

For general information on our other products and services or for technical support, please contact our Customer Care Department within the United States at (800) 762-2974, outside the United States at (317) 572-3993 or fax (317) 572-4002.

Wiley publishes in a variety of print and electronic formats and by print-on-demand. Some material included with standard print versions of this book may not be included in e-books or in print-on-demand. If this book refers to media such as a CD or DVD that is not included in the version you purchased, you may download this material at http://booksupport.wiley.com. For more information about Wiley products, visit www.wiley.com.

Library of Congress Cataloging-in-Publication Data is Available:
ISBN 9781119687016 (Hardcover)
ISBN 9781119686903 (ePDF)
ISBN 9781119686972 (ePub)

Cover Design: Wiley

SKY10022985_120320

CONTENTS

Contents

Contents

Contents

PREFACE

The Premise and the Promise

The premise of *Everyday People, Extraordinary Leadership: How to Make a Difference Regardless of Your Title, Role, or Authority* is quite simple: leadership is a learnable set of actions and behaviors that is available to everyone. In the pages that follow, we make the case that leadership is not about rank, position, or authority, and we will provide data to support this claim. We'll also share examples of individuals who, as a result of engaging in practices of exemplary leadership, have guided others in making extraordinary things happen in their organizations and communities.

Everyday People, Extraordinary Leadership is about what *individuals* do to effect change and improvement. It is about the behaviors and actions individuals use to transform values into actions, visions into realities, obstacles into innovations, division into unity, and risks into rewards. It's about exercising leadership that contributes to creating an environment in which people can work together to turn perplexing problems and challenging opportunities into remarkable successes.

All too often, when leadership is discussed within workplaces and communities, attention is given primarily to those appointed or elected to positions of authority. While leaders with titles certainly deserve credit for what they do, they are not the only people who matter. In fact, we would argue that there are just as many, probably even more, leaders without titles who contribute to collective achievements and well-being. Workplace and community engagement are not just a function of what formal leaders do; they are also related to how *all* leaders in organizations behave.

The COVID-19 pandemic is a case in point as it spread across the globe, overwhelming healthcare systems, shutting down a significant number of commerce and educational systems, and totally disrupting the normal way of life for effectively every person on the planet. It has been an unprecedented crisis like no other experienced in our lifetime. While there are—and have to be—global, national, regional, state, and local coordinated efforts to address the pandemic, it is also the many small acts of leadership among doctors, nurses, first responders, teachers, parents, students, volunteers, and other concerned citizens that make a difference. They create novel ways to treat the sick, care for the vulnerable, deal with shortages, produce personal protective equipment, recognize heroes, and even bring a bit of joy to an otherwise tragic and depressing situation.

Another case in point about how tragedy and adversity create opportunities for people to step up and lead, and that leadership arises as much, if not more so, from the bottom up as it does from the top down, is the response to the death of George Floyd while in police custody. His death was the tipping point in long-standing tensions around matters of racial and social justice and police treatment of people of color. Within a day of the event, protests began, first in Minneapolis, where the incident occurred, and then across the United States and in major cities around the world. These were mostly decentralized actions initiated largely by young people of highly diverse backgrounds who had no formal titles or positions. They captured the attention of governments, businesses, and ordinary citizens and supercharged calls for more diversity, equity, and inclusion in every institution.

There continues to be no shortage of challenges facing individuals, organizations, and communities, and no limits to the opportunities and needs for people to lead. We wrote this book to help you prepare to become the best leader you can be and take advantage of the chances you have to make this world a little bit better place than you find it.

Who Should Read This Book?

This book is for and about people who do not have titles, like supervisor, manager, executive, chief, head, director, captain, boss, and the like, or some formal authority over other people. It's intended for front-line workers, new hires, individual contributors, salespeople, analysts, researchers, consultants, professionals, community activists, volunteers, project leads, scientists, engineers, administrators, artists, athletes, attorneys, programmers, coaches, teachers, parents, and all the others who lead without the benefit of hierarchical position or rank. The book aims to help people—no matter their role—strengthen their capacity to make extraordinary things happen.

We also wrote this book to uplift your spirits. We will show you how you can be effective at leading without any formal authority. Leadership matters from wherever you do it. We have learned from our research—which is discussed in each chapter—that people who aren't managers or executives are far more capable of developing themselves as leaders and exercising leadership than tradition or myth has ever assumed possible.

Managers, executives, and leadership developers will benefit, as well, from reading this book. They will find here example after example of people who have made extraordinary things happen without having the advantage of title or positional power. We hope that it will reinforce the need for them to provide leadership development opportunities to *everyone* in their organization—and much sooner in people's careers than they typically do. We know that the best leaders are the best learners, and learning leadership is best begun *before* people join the workforce or take on formal or official organizational responsibilities.

As you will see from the scores of examples in this book, the principles apply regardless of the nature of your organization, and they are not dependent upon any particular demographic characteristic (e.g., age, gender, ethnicity, function, nationality, etc.) or personality variable. The focus is on the behaviors and actions of what people do when they are exercising exemplary leadership.

Research-Based Practices

The principles and practices described in *Everyday People, Extraordinary Leadership* are based solidly on quantitative and qualitative research. The book has its origins in a study we began in 1983. We wanted to know what people did when they were at their "personal best" in leading others. People see their individual leadership standards of excellence in these experiences. We started with an assumption that to discover best practices we did not have to interview and survey star performers, select celebrities, or people "at the top." Instead, we assumed that by asking people at all levels and across a broad array of organizational settings to describe extraordinary experiences, we would be able to find and identify patterns of success. And we did.

The results of our initial investigation—and of the ongoing research we have conducted for nearly four decades—have been striking in their consistency and are a refutation of many leader stereotypes. People frequently assume, for example, that leadership is different from one type of organization or culture to the next. Nothing could be further from the truth. While each setting may look different from the outside, we find that what leaders do when they are at their best is quite similar. This pattern of behavior varies little across locations and circumstances. It's true enough that the context keeps evolving, and the landscape of workplaces, communities, and countries has shifted over time, but leadership remains an understandable and generalizable process. While each leader is a unique individual, there are shared patterns to the practice of leadership. In each chapter of this book, you will find empirical evidence that shows the positive difference leaders without titles make across a wide spectrum of settings.

You can find out more about how we conducted the research for this book in the Appendix. Details about the research methodology, including psychometric properties of the *Leadership Practices Inventory* and analytics, as well as highlights of validation studies by various independent scholars are available on our website: www.leadershipchallenge.com. Those interested in broadening their perspective on leadership should look at some of our other leadership books, such as *Credibility: How Leaders Gain and Lose It, Why People Demand It*; *The Truth About Leadership: The No-Fads, Heart-of-the-Matter Facts You Need to Know*; and *Learning Leadership: The Five Fundamentals of Becoming an Exemplary Leader*.

A Guidebook on Leadership

Consider *Everyday People, Extraordinary Leadership* as a guidebook to take along on your leadership journey. We have designed it to describe what leaders do, explain the fundamental principles that support these leadership practices, and provide actual case examples of real people in the workplace or community who demonstrate each practice. Based on the real-world experiences of thousands of people who have answered the call for leadership, we offer specific recommendations on what you can do to make these practices your own and to continue your leadership development.

Chapter 1 introduces you to our point of view about leadership—specifically that leadership is not a position, hierarchical place, or genetic trait. We discuss leadership as a relationship, and we reveal who is at the top of the list of leadership role models. We describe the characteristics that people most desire in their leaders and present the foundation on which all great leadership is built. We briefly describe The Five Practices of Exemplary

Leadership® revealed in our research. We tell the leadership story from the inside and move outward, describing leadership first as a personal journey of exploration and then as a mobilization of others. The research shows that leadership is not the private reserve of a few charismatic men and women, but instead a learnable set of behaviors and actions people use when they are bringing forth the best from themselves and others.

In Chapters 2 through 6 we explore each of The Five Practices, one to a chapter, and demonstrate that taken together they provide an operating system for leadership. Once you understand the "operating system," you can create and run any number of different applications off of it, akin to what an operating system provides for computer software. Discussions build on the results of our original research, buttressed by studies from other scholars, and provide a particular point of view on leadership that is empirically sound and practically useful. Case examples and empirical evidence generously illustrate each leadership practice and document how using more of each practice yields more favorable outcomes. Each chapter has recommended actions, concluding with two specific first steps that you should take to put the leadership practice to use in developing your leadership capabilities.

In Chapter 7, we share some concluding research on how leadership matters not only to your colleagues or community, but also to you personally. We discuss six fundamentals for learning leadership, and explore three basic types of learning opportunities. In so doing we aim to demystify leadership and show how every person has the capacity to learn to lead. Finally, we advise that the process of becoming the best leader you can be will fundamentally change who you are and how you present yourself day in and day out. To that end, we offer a concluding reflective activity to help you get started on the next stage of your leadership journey.

The Future of Leadership

The domain of leaders is the future. We hope this book contributes to the ongoing revitalization of the workplace, to the renewal of healthy communities, and to greater respect and understanding among people of all traditions. We fervently hope that it enriches your life and the lives of your colleagues, your friends, and family. The most significant contribution you can make as a leader is to strengthen others so they can adapt, grow, and flourish.

Leadership matters. It's essential in every sector, in every community, and in every country. In these times of unprecedented change, organizations and communities need more leaders, and now more than ever they need leaders who can unite and mobilize others in a common cause.

So much extraordinary work needs to be done, and you have the opportunity to make a meaningful difference in how it is done. Accept the challenge to learn to become the best leader you can be—for the sake of your community, your workplace, and for those you love.

James M. Kouzes
Barry Z. Posner
November 2020

CHAPTER 1

Leadership Is Not a Position

WHEN YOU HEAR the word "leader," what immediately comes to mind?

Maybe you think of someone with a title, such as CEO, president, prime minister, or admiral. Maybe you think of some famous public figure, such as a celebrity actor or singer, start-up founder, or pro athlete. Maybe you think of someone from the history books who led a revolution, conquest, or world-changing movement. Or maybe you think of someone who created a breakthrough invention, won the Nobel or Pulitzer Prize, wrote a best-selling novel or Grammy-winning song. It's rather common to see these kinds of responses. They are reinforced every time you read one of those lists of the "50 Greatest Leaders of the Year." In fact, if you take a look at one of the most well-known lists, you'll see that 100 percent of the so-called "greatest leaders" fall into these categories.[1] It's true for young leaders as well. In a list of young global leaders prepared by the World Economic Forum, 85 percent of the young leaders held the title of a senior executive, founder, or government official.[2] The majority of "leaders" who make these lists and are featured in the popular press are people with titles and at the apex of their organizations.

It's not that these individuals aren't leaders. They are. It's just that they are *not* the *only* leaders on the planet. In fact, they aren't even the majority of leaders. We've collected data from millions of people around the world and we can report, without a doubt, that there are leaders everywhere. There are leaders in every profession, discipline, and field, in every type of organization and industry, every religion, and every country; you find them from young to old, male, female, and gender nonconforming, across every ethnic and cultural category. Leaders are not just found at the top of organizations; they abound at all levels, including the middle, as well as on the front lines. There are leaders outside of formal organizations, too, in neighborhoods, community associations, clubs, sports teams, and families.

You could have a title like manager, director, or vice president. You could have people who report to you directly, but these would not necessarily make you a leader. Titles are granted, but being a leader is something that you earn, and you earn it not by your place in the organization but by how you behave. And through your behavior, you earn recognition as a leader in the eyes of those around you, and in the relationships you have with them. Indeed, it's much more likely that you are a leader who is a parent, coach, teacher, frontline worker, project manager, volunteer, community activist, or concerned citizen. You could also be a leader who is an individual contributor, professional, volunteer, analyst, consultant, representative, administrator, engineer, or scientist. You don't have to be at the top to lead; you can lead from any position or place.

So let's get something straight right from the start. Leadership is *not* a hierarchical level. It is not a title or a rank. It is not a position of power or a place of privilege. When you look up the word *leadership* in the dictionary it does not start with an uppercase *L*. It starts with a lowercase *l*, and *lead, leader,* and *leadership* literally derive from the word meaning "to go" or "to guide." That's what leadership is all about: going places and guiding others.

From whom do people seek this kind of guidance and direction? We decided to find out.

Leadership Is a Relationship

In a global study involving over 35,000 people, we asked them to think about the individuals in their lives who were their role models for leadership.[3] We provided a number of categories from which their leadership role model might come. Take a look at the list in Table 1.1. From which category is the one person whom you would choose as your leadership role model?

Whom did you select? When thinking back over their lives and selecting their most important leadership role models, respondents overwhelmingly nominated a family member more often than anyone else. Next most important were a teacher or coach and an immediate supervisor. Those under 25 years of age (Gen Z) had these ranked second and third, while Millennials (Gen Y and Gen X; ages 25 to 55) and Boomers

TABLE 1.1 Leadership Role Models
• Actor or Entertainer
• Business Leader
• Coach
• Community Leader
• Co-Worker/Colleagues
• Family Members
• Immediate Supervisor
• Religious Leader
• Political Leader
• Professional Athlete
• Teacher
• None/Not sure

(56 and older) had them ranked in the reverse order. For those in the workplace, their teachers and coaches are their immediate supervisors. Another 6 percent indicated a co-worker or colleague. Altogether these four categories accounted for more than three-quarters of all responses. Eight percent indicated "none/not sure," which meant that only 16 percent of all responses were in the categories of business leader, community leader, political leader, religious leader, actor or entertainer, and professional athlete. This pattern is relatively stable across genders, ethnic groups, educational levels, industries, professions, and even hierarchical levels.

The data clearly shows that the people selected are individuals respondents are closest to. They are not the people in the news, on TV, or in social media. They're the ones with whom people have had the most frequent contact. In other words, leadership role models are *local*. While famous folks may occupy the headlines, those with whom you have more personal contact are most likely to become your role models and have more influence over how you lead and how you develop as a leader. And make no mistake about it, the same realization applies to you. You very well could be the leadership role model for those closest to you—more than could someone on that so-called list of the world's best leaders.

These results have extremely important implications. Parents, teachers, and coaches are the individuals who are setting the leadership example for young people. It's not hip-hop artists, movie stars, professional athletes, or others making news on social media who inspire them about leadership. And if you are a parent, a teacher, or volunteer coach, *you* are the one they are most likely going to look to for the example of how a leader responds to competitive situations, handles crises, deals with loss, or resolves ethical dilemmas. It's not someone else. It's *you*.

The findings also reveal that if you're in a work organization, you are more likely to find role models among your colleagues on your immediate team than at the pinnacle of the organization or somewhere on the outside. If you are now a supervisor or manager, *you* may already be someone's role model. You are more likely than any other person in the organization to influence their desire to stay or leave, the trajectory of their careers, their ethical behavior, their ability to perform at their best, their drive to wow customers, and their motivation to share and serve the organization's vision and values.

There's no escape. To some, *you* are or could be their role model for leading. Those individuals could be colleagues on your team, they could be peers in another part of your workplace, they could be kids on the youth athletic team or club you coach after work, they could be people from your community who are working with you as a volunteer, or it could be your son or daughter, spouse or partner, at home.

A question for you to consider: If you are potentially a role model for someone, wouldn't you want to be the best role model you can be? It's your choice. Just be aware that regardless of title or position, be it at home, in school, the community, or workplace, you must take responsibility for the quality of leadership the people around you observe and receive. You are accountable to yourself and others for the leadership you demonstrate.

The individuals selected most frequently as leadership role models—family members, teachers, coaches, immediate supervisors, and co-workers—also make evident the most important finding of all. They underscore the truth that *leadership is a relationship*. Leadership is a relationship between those who aspire to lead and those who choose to follow. This is true regardless of whether the relationship is one-to-one or one-to-many. If you are going to be a leader whose guidance others want to follow willingly, there must be a human connection, something that binds you and others together. It's the quality of this relationship that will determine over the long term whether others will follow your lead or not. To lead effectively, you have to appreciate the underlying dynamics of the leader-constituent relationship. It's extremely important to understand, therefore, the qualities that people look for in the leaders they would *willingly* follow. If people are going to want to follow you over the course of a project or the course of a career, what do they *most* want to see in your behavior?

A relationship between people characterized by fear and distrust will never produce anything of lasting value. A relationship characterized by mutual respect and confidence will overcome the greatest adversities and leave a legacy of significance. Any discussion of leadership must attend to the dynamics of this relationship. Strategies, tactics, skills, and techniques are empty without an understanding of the essential human aspirations that connect people with their leaders and leaders with their people.

Credibility Is the Foundation of Leadership

What sort of person would you listen to, take advice from, be influenced by, and willingly follow, not because you have to, but because you want to? What does it take for you to be the kind of person that others want to follow, doing so enthusiastically and voluntarily? Understanding and responding to these expectations is essential to the exercise of exemplary leadership.

To understand this leader-constituent relationship we have routinely been conducting surveys over the past 40 years about the personal values, traits, and characteristics that people indicate are most important to them in an individual they would willingly follow. A key word in this sentence is "willingly." It is one thing to follow someone because you think you have to "or else," and it's another when you follow an individual because you want to.

We've gathered responses from more than 120,000 respondents, and they have been striking in their consistency over the years.[4] Our evidence shows that people must pass several essential character tests before they earn the designation of leader from other people, as demonstrated by the data presented in Table 1.2.

All the characteristics receive votes, and therefore each one is important to at least some individuals. What is most evident, however, is that over time, across continents, demographic, and organizational differences, only four have continuously received the majority (over 60 percent) of the preferences. What people most look for and admire in a leader has been constant. If people are going to follow someone willingly, they must believe the individual is honest, competent, inspiring, and forward-looking.

TABLE 1.2 Personal Values, Traits, and Characteristics That People Look for in Their Leaders*	
Value, Trait, or Characteristic	**Percentage of Respondents Selecting This Category***
Honest (truthful, has integrity, trustworthy, has character, ethical)	87
Forward-looking (visionary, foresighted, concerned about the future, has sense of direction)	69
Competent (capable, proficient, effective, gets the job done, professional)	67
Inspiring (uplifting, enthusiastic, energetic, optimistic, positive about future)	66
Intelligent (bright, smart, intellectual, logical)	45
Broad-minded (open-minded, flexible, receptive, tolerant)	38
Dependable (reliable, conscientious, responsible)	34
Supportive (helpful, offers assistance, comforting)	36
Fair-minded (just, unprejudiced, objective, forgiving)	40
Straightforward (direct, candid, forthright)	34
Cooperative (collaborative, team player, responsive)	27

(Continued)

TABLE 1.2 (Continued)	
Value, Trait, or Characteristic	Percentage of Respondents Selecting This Category*
Courageous (bold, daring, gutsy)	24
Caring (appreciative, compassionate, concerned, loving, nurturing)	22
Determined (dedicated, resolute, persistent, purposeful)	22
Imaginative (creative, innovative, curious)	22
Ambitious (aspiring, hard-working, striving)	19
Mature (experienced, wise, has depth)	16
Loyal (faithful, dutiful, unswerving in allegiance, devoted)	15
Self-controlled (restrained, self-disciplined)	10
Independent (self-reliant, self-sufficient, self-confident)	6

* Note that several synonyms are included in each category.

While the fact that what people look for in their leaders has remained consistent over time, despite the ever-shifting forces affecting economic and social life, there is another profound implication revealed by this data. These survey results have a solid conceptual foundation in what social psychologists and communications experts refer to as "source credibility."

In assessing the believability of sources of information—whether newscasters, salespeople, physicians, or priests; whether business executives, military officers, politicians, or civic leaders—researchers typically evaluate them on their perceived trustworthiness, expertise, and dynamism. The more highly people are rated on these three dimensions the more credible they are perceived as sources of information.[5]

Notice how remarkably similar these three characteristics are to the essential qualities people want from their leaders—honest, competent, and inspiring—three of the top four items selected in our surveys. Link the theory to this data, and the striking conclusion is that people want to follow leaders who, more than anything, are credible. *Credibility is the foundation of leadership.* People must be able, above all else, to believe in their leaders. To willingly follow them, people must believe that the leaders' word can be trusted, that they are personally passionate and enthusiastic about the work, and that they have the knowledge and skill to lead.[6]

If you are going to ask others to follow you to some uncertain future, and if the journey is going to require hardships and possibly sacrifices, then it is imperative that people believe in you. People must be able to believe that your words can be trusted, that you will do what you say, that you are personally excited and enthusiastic about the direction in which the group is headed, and that you have the knowledge and skills to lead.

This all leads to the *First Law of Leadership*: *If people don't believe in the messenger, they won't believe the message.*

The Five Practices of Exemplary Leadership

So what is it that leaders do to build and sustain credibility? What do they do that makes others see them as capable and trustworthy leaders? What are the behaviors that people exhibit that engage and mobilize others to want to follow? What are people actually *doing* when they are leading and making extraordinary things happen?

? Question to leaders

To answer these questions, we have been asking people since the early 1980s to tell us what they did when they were at their "personal best" as leaders. We continue to ask this question in our studies and workshops around the world. We have collected thousands of Personal-Best Leadership Experiences—stories about times when individuals report how they excelled at leading, when they were operating at peak performance—from across a wide variety of settings, nationalities, organizations, levels, ages, genders, educational backgrounds, and the like. We've interviewed students in universities, individual contributors at work, middle managers in large and small companies, volunteers in the community, and executives in the C-suite about times when they excelled at leading—when they were doing their best as leaders.

Before finding out what others said, reflect for a moment on something that *you* would consider your Personal-Best Leadership Experience. This experience could be a time when you emerged as the informal leader, or it could be a time when you were appointed to take on the lead role in a new project. It could be in any functional area, in any type of organization, in a staff or line role. The experience does not need to be in your current organization. It could be in a prior job, a club, a community volunteer setting, a professional organization, a school, a team, a congregation, or even a family setting. It could be a project to improve a product or service, an initiative to bring about a change in your neighborhood, the turnaround of a poorly performing team, the start-up of a new business, jumping in during a crisis, or any other kind of challenge that required leadership.

When we initially analyzed the themes in the thousands of personal-best stories we had collected, two meta-lessons emerged and continue to be front and center. The first lesson we learned is that *everyone has a story to tell*. Regardless of whom we ask, people are able to identify a time when they did their best as a leader. The specifics of the personal-best stories varied from person to person because the individuals responding to the Personal-Best Leadership Experience Questionnaire were different from one another along a myriad of factors. Despite any individual differences, settings, and circumstances, the second lesson we learned is that the actions and behaviors of leaders when at their best are *more similar than they are different*. There is a set of *common behaviors and actions* that people demonstrate when they operate at their personal-best as leaders. These behaviors are universal, and they have stood the test of time and place.[7] Moreover, hundreds of independent scholars have validated this framework in their own studies investigating the central role leadership plays in personal well-being, organizational productivity, and effectiveness.[8] The evidence is clear: exemplary leadership is found in every corner of the globe, every sector of society, every community, every organization, and every type of individual.

We've grouped these behaviors into a *leadership operating system* that we call The Five Practices of Exemplary Leadership.[9] When making extraordinary things happen, leaders:

- ► Model the Way
- ► Inspire a Shared Vision
- ► Challenge the Process
- ► Enable Others to Act
- ► Encourage the Heart

Let's take a brief look now at each of The Five Practices. We will explore them more completely in Chapters 2 through 6. In those chapters you will find numerous stories and examples about how people much like you have applied them in their settings. We'll also provide several practical ideas about how you can learn to be the best leader you can be.

Model the Way   Titles are granted, but it's your behavior that earns you respect. This sentiment was expressed in everyone's personal-best case, as represented by such comments as "I couldn't tell anyone what to do, I had to show them," "I had to be a role model for the behavior I wanted from others," and "I had to be clear about my personal values and then make sure that I walked the talk." Exemplary leaders know that if they want to earn the respect of the people around them and achieve the highest standards, they must be models of the behavior they expect of others. Exemplary leaders *Model the Way*.

To effectively model the way, you first must be clear about your guiding principles. You must *clarify values by finding your voice*. When you understand who you are and the values you hold dear, then you can speak authentically about the beliefs that you want to guide your decisions and actions. But *your* values aren't the only values that matter. Leaders don't speak just for themselves. They also speak for the group, and in every team, organization, and community, there are others who also feel strongly about matters of principle. As a leader, you also must help identify and *affirm the shared values* of the group you are working with. Without an agreed-on and collective understanding of what is right and what is wrong, then anything goes, and there are neither practical nor ethical standards for people to follow.

When it comes to determining how serious leaders are about what they say, however, a leader's actions are far more important than their words. People listen to the talk, and then they watch the walk. Words and actions must be consistent for leaders to be believed, so exemplary leaders *set the example by aligning actions with shared values*. The best way that you prove that something is important is by doing it yourself. Through daily actions, leaders demonstrate their deep commitment to their beliefs and to the shared values of the groups they are part of.

Inspire a Shared Vision People describe their Personal-Best Leadership Experiences as times when they imagined exciting and meaningful futures for themselves and others. They reported actions such as: "I told the team that we need everyone's commitment to make our vision a reality, to reach our dreams and make them happen," "The more I imagined what was possible, the more clearly I could describe what the future might hold in store for all of us," and "We had to be aligned so that we could find a common purpose as a team going forward." They had a desire to create something that no one else had ever created before. They had visions of what could be, and they had absolute faith and confidence that those aspirations could become reality. When performing at their best, leaders *Inspire a Shared Vision.*

In many ways, leaders live their lives backward. By building upon experiences, they see pictures in their mind's eye of what success will look like even before they've started their projects, much as architects draw blueprints or engineers build models. Their clear image of the future pulls them forward, and they are able to speak enthusiastically and energetically about the compelling possibilities. They *envision the future by imagining exciting and ennobling possibilities.*

Yet visions seen only by leaders are insufficient to create an organized movement or a significant change. People will not follow until they can embrace a vision as their own. They must be able to see exciting possibilities for themselves. To realize a vision, then, leaders have to be clear not only about why it is important to them, but they must be equally clear about why it is important to those they lead. To perform at their best, leaders *enlist others in a common vision by appealing to shared ideals and aspirations.*

When you truly understand and take to heart the hopes and dreams of those you are involved with, you can breathe life into the aspirations of others. You are able to forge a unity of purpose by explaining and showing how and why the dream is for the common good. The way you ignite passion in others is by expressing contagious enthusiasm for the compelling vision of the group, communicating their zeal through vivid language and an expressive style.

Challenge the Process   Every single personal-best leadership case involved some change from the status quo. Not one person claimed to achieve a personal best by keeping things the same, doing what had always been done. They said: "I needed to change the business-as-usual climate by finding ways to experiment and learn," "We began by brainstorming what we would change if anything was possible," and "We found that big things are done by doing lots of small things." This is why leaders *Challenge the Process.*

Challenge is the crucible for greatness. It provides the context in which adversity and vision interact to provide for the creation of something new. When at their best leaders are pioneers. They are willing to step out into the unknown and continuously *search for opportunities by seizing the initiative and by looking outward for innovative ways to improve.*

While they are proactive, leaders aren't the only creators or originators of new programs, services, or processes. In fact, it's more likely that they're not. Innovation comes more from listening than from telling—more from asking questions and hearing what others are thinking and have to say. When challenging the process, your primary contributions are often the recognition of good ideas, the support of those ideas, and the willingness to challenge the system to get new products, processes, services, and systems adopted.

We also found that in the Personal-Best Leadership Experiences, leaders had to *experiment and take risks by continually generating small wins and learning from experience.* Leaders know well that innovation and change all involve trial and error. One way you can deal with these potential risks and failures is to approach change through incremental steps. Little victories, when piled on top of each other, build confidence that people can meet even the most significant challenges. In making those victories possible, you strengthen commitment to the long-term future.

Learning also unlocks the door to progress, and exemplary leaders make a point to ask "What can we learn?" when things don't go as expected. The best leaders are the best learners, treating every experiment, every innovation, and every mistake as an opportunity to develop and grow.

Enable Others to Act   Leaders know they can't do it alone. Grand dreams don't become significant realities through the actions of a single person. In their personal-best cases, they showed their appreciation of this truth with statements such as: "It was necessary to take into consideration each person's perspectives and ensure that the decisions were made by the team and not individual decisions," "The key was building relationships with people who were needed to help us make this happen," and "Giving them the space and latitude to do their work gave them the confidence to do what hadn't been done before." Leadership is a team effort, not a solo performance, and to make extraordinary things happen in organizations exemplary leaders *Enable Others to Act*.

Leaders proudly discussed how they had to *foster collaboration by building a climate of trust and facilitating relationships*. They engage all those who were necessary to make the project work, and develop collaborative relationships with colleagues. They are considerate of the needs and interests of others. They bring people together, creating an atmosphere where people understand they have a shared fate and that they should treat others as they would like to be treated. They make sure that everyone wins.

This experience underscores how the work of leaders is making people feel strong, capable, and committed. Leaders *strengthen others by increasing self-determination and developing competence and confidence*. People don't stick around for very long or perform at their best if their leader makes them feel weak, dependent, or alienated. People will give their all when you can strengthen their belief that they can do more than they ever thought possible. In fact, it was not unusual for people to indicate that when working with their best leaders, they gave more than 100 percent of themselves to the endeavor because that leader was able to bring out from them more than what they themselves had imagined. When people have confidence in you and your relationship with them is based on trust they are most willing to take risks, make changes, and maintain forward momentum.

Encourage the Heart   The climb to the top of any new and challenging endeavor is arduous and steep, and it is not surprising that people can become exhausted, frustrated, and disenchanted. Leaders indicated in their Personal-Best Leadership Experiences that they had to *Encourage the Heart* of those with whom they were working to carry on, especially when they might have been tempted to give up. They said things such as: "You have to show people that you care about them as people and how they are capable of doing a lot more than they think," "Praise and encouragement are the best gifts because people need to have their hard work and efforts acknowledged, to know that they are making a difference," and "We were generous with compliments and this allowed us to feel good about ourselves, and when you feel good you are more productive."

Genuine acts of caring, whether exhibited in dramatic gestures or simple actions, uplift people's spirits and keep them motivated. It is part of a leader's job to *recognize contributions by showing appreciation for individual excellence.* Over the years, we've seen thousands of examples of individual recognition and group celebration, from handwritten thank-you notes to marching bands and biopic video ceremonies. But recognition and celebration aren't about fun and games—though both abound when leaders encourage the hearts of their constituents. Encouraging the heart is also not about orchestrating formal awards ceremonies or throwing parties designed to create some artificial sense of camaraderie. It is about *celebrating the values and the victories by creating a spirit of community.* Public encouragement is valuable because it's how you visibly reinforce what's important and show appreciation for actions that support the team's values. Whether striving to raise quality standards, recover from disaster, or make a dramatic change of any kind, people must see the benefit of aligning behavior with cherished values. When celebrations and rituals are done with authenticity and from the heart, you build a strong sense of collective identity and community spirit that can carry a group through tough times.

These five leadership practices—Model the Way, Inspire a Shared Vision, Challenge the Process, Enable Others to Act, and Encourage the Heart—do not represent an ideology or theory about leadership so much as they provide an operating system for what it means to be practicing leadership and making a difference. Engaging in any of the behaviors associated with The Five Practices does not necessitate any particular personality or require any specific demographic characteristics or advanced educational degrees. There's a very good chance that you are already leading; you just might not recognize that you are doing it. Or perhaps you don't believe you can exercise leadership and don't see yourself as a leader; in that case, there's a very good chance that what you think you can't do, you won't do.

You Are Already Leading

Another essential lesson we learned when analyzing Personal-Best Leadership Experiences is that leadership is a set of *behaviors and actions* that are available to everyone. Leadership is *not* some mystical quality or the private reserve of a special class of charismatic people. It is not a gene or a trait in the DNA of a blessed few. It is not a single personality characteristic or a special innate talent that some people have and others do not. It is not a singular strength, and it is not a gift from the gods.

We repeat: Leadership is a set of behaviors and actions that are available to everyone. Let's check out that claim! For each of the questions below, please answer "yes" or "no." Have you ever:

yes ▸ Spoken about one or more values that you hold dear?

yes ▸ Set a personal example of what you wanted someone else to do?

yes ▸ Talked excitedly about something that might be possible, even though it didn't exist today?

yes ▸ Asked someone else to go along with you to do something?

yes ▸ Tried to make something work better than it was currently?

NO ▸ Been one of the first people to try something new or different from what you were used to doing?

yes ▸ Listened intently to someone else's point of view, someone you didn't necessary agree with?

yes ▸ Helped someone else learn how to do an assignment or work better?

yes ▸ Said "thank you" to another person for a job done well?

yes ▸ Taken part in a celebration recognizing the accomplishment of a colleague?

These are just some of the actions that leaders take day-in and day-out when at their best, and if you answered "yes" to many or most of the questions above, then congratulations because this means *you are already leading.* Maybe you are not leading frequently enough, but you are leading. On the other hand, if you answered "no" to most of these questions, we think you'll agree that all of them are actions you could take if you were convinced that doing so would be beneficial, resulting in greater well-being and productivity for yourself and others.

Leadership is in the actions that you take. It emerges from the values that guide your decisions and behavior. It results from the visions you have for yourself and others. It is evident in the changes you initiate and the challenges you accept. It appears in the trust you build and the connections you strengthen. It's about how you lift others up and how you make others feel valued.

Even though we can demonstrate to you that leadership is something you—and others—can do, leadership myths persist. And clearly those myths include believing that leadership comes with a title or position, that it requires a set of direct reports, and that leadership is some genetic quality that is in short supply. Becoming an exemplary leader begins with the *belief* that everyone is capable of leadership and that you can be a better leader than you are right now because you can learn to improve your skills and abilities. It is also essential that you believe that your actions matter and that leadership makes a difference.

Leadership Makes a Difference

Exemplary leadership makes a significant difference in people's levels of well-being, commitment, and motivation, their work performance, and the success of their organizations. That's the definitive conclusion from analyzing data from over three million respondents around the world using the *Leadership Practices Inventory* to assess how often people engage in The Five Practices of Exemplary Leadership.[10] Those leaders who most frequently use The Five Practices are considerably more effective across a variety of outcomes than their counterparts who use them less often.

Looking at the data just for those people who indicate they are "individual contributors" (as opposed to executives, middle managers, or supervisors) reveals the same pattern as these overall findings. In each of the subsequent chapters we present empirical evidence from their peers that further substantiates these results.* For example, there is a very strong correlation ($r = .67$) between the likelihood of "being recommended to colleagues as a good leader" by one's peers and the frequency to which they observe the individual engaging in The Five Practices. As shown in Figure 1, the more frequently that one's colleagues and co-workers observe that person engaging in The Five Practices, the more strongly they agree that that individual is a good leader. This certainly makes sense. You can't be regarded as a leader if you don't behave as a leader.

So you don't have to be in a leadership position or have direct reports in order to make a difference to your colleagues and co-workers or to be seen as most effective by your manager. The bottom line empirically is that the more you utilize The Five Practices of Exemplary Leadership, the more likely it is that you'll have a positive influence on other people and the organization. That's what all our data and the scores of research conducted by independent scholars[11] add up to: If you want to have a significant impact on the people around you and the organizations you are involved with, you'd be wise to invest in learning the behaviors that enable you to become the very best leader you can.

While The Five Practices of Exemplary Leadership don't *completely* explain why leaders and their organizations are successful—which is actually good news because you should be very skeptical of anyone who promises perfection or offers a money-back guarantee—it is clear that engaging in them makes quite a difference no matter who you are,

---

* Unless otherwise indicated, when we refer to "data" we are using the results from the sample and analysis described in the Appendix. The sample generally involves the independent viewpoints of the co-workers and colleagues who were asked to provide feedback on the leadership behaviors of one of their peers. They completed the Observer version of the *Leadership Practices Inventory*, provided demographic information, answered various questions regarding their workplace attitudes, and offered assessment of the leadership effectiveness of their peer.

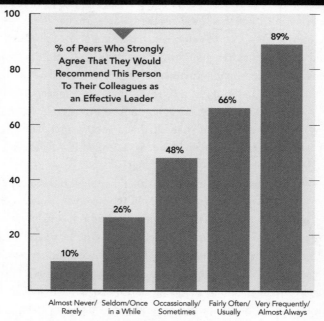

Figure 1 Likelihood of Being Recommended as a Good Leader by Peers Increases with Greater Frequency of Leadership Practices

% of Peers Who Strongly Agree That They Would Recommend This Person To Their Colleagues as an Effective Leader

Frequency with Which Individual Engages in The Five Practices of Exemplary Leadership

what you do, or where you are located. How you behave as a leader matters, and it matters a lot. *You* are the leader who makes the most difference in the lives of those you lead. And you are the one who has to determine how to match these practices and their associated behaviors to the settings and circumstances that you face. That's how you combine the art of leadership with mastery of the science of leadership.

In the next five chapters are detailed descriptions of what people do to Model the Way, Inspire a Shared Vision, Challenge the Process, Enable Others to Act, and Encourage the Heart. You will find stories and examples of people just like you who demonstrate each of these leadership practices, and we provide ideas, tools, and techniques that you can use on your leadership development journey.

As you read each of the chapters, keep in mind the key messages from this overview of our research on what people are doing when they are leading:

- ▶ Leadership is not a position or hierarchical place or genetic trait
- ▶ Leadership is a relationship
- ▶ Leadership role models are local
- ▶ Leadership is everyone's business
- ▶ Credibility is the foundation of leadership
- ▶ Leadership is an understandable, observable, and learnable set of behaviors and actions
- ▶ You are already leading . . . and you can exercise leadership more frequently
- ▶ Leadership makes a difference
- ▶ You make a difference

In the next chapter we explain how you begin to earn the trust of the people around you. We show how you Model the Way by clarifying values and setting an example for others.

CHAPTER 2

Model the Way

ERIN BYRNE MCELROY keeps herself very busy. She works in business development and brand engagement in a manufacturing firm, volunteers regularly with local nonprofits and civic organizations in her rural suburban county in the Midwest, and enjoys daily activities with her family. But in March 2020, like everyone else in her community, Erin was ordered to shelter-in-place due to the COVID-19 pandemic. She found it hard to sit still.

As someone deeply involved with her community, the pandemic caused Erin to wonder how local businesses would adapt, and she worried about the health of frontline workers who were caring for others and unable to shelter-in-place. Wanting to do something to help, she reflected on the values that mattered the most to her: "I returned to my core values and took an internal audit of my heart and mind." "Service to others" was most important to her, along with warmth, graciousness, gratitude, connection, kindness, and being the difference. But how could she put these values into practice during a pandemic?

Erin thought there might be a way to achieve a doubly impactful objective—supporting the local restaurants and at the same time feeding frontline workers. Knowing she couldn't achieve this goal alone, she called up four close advisors and confidants—Rod Crandall, Anne Marie

Brown, Devon Tessmer, and Alexandra Eesley—with whom she had collaborated in various community activities throughout the years. She had found that while "we were different in personalities and professional talents, I knew that servant leadership was in their hearts." Erin felt aligned with them on a common set of values and beliefs, and she wanted their counsel on how to be of service to others during the pandemic.

What emerged from their conversations was a "simple act of kindness," which they named Project Front Line. They created a GoFundMe campaign and the team reached out to the community, through social media, asking, "Do you have a love of local restaurants, cafes, and bakeries? Do you want to lift up the front lines that are going to be out there fighting this?" Erin and her colleagues vetted applications from restaurants, bakeries, and other food service companies, and signed them up to prepare meals for hospitals, urgent care centers, nursing homes/rehab centers, pharmacies, and first responders. Erin set the example by being the first to donate.

Because of the shelter-in-place orders, Erin harnessed the power of connectivity to lead remotely. She led a weekly virtual meeting to coordinate activities like deliveries, meal preparations, marketing, and public relations. Every morning and every night Erin carved out space for virtual tasks such as posting photo images and comments about the positive impact the project was having. She thanked each donor and replied to social media comments and direct messages, as well as emails from people in other communities about how they could do something similar. Her communications with various media outlets lead to stories published about the project and the people being served. Erin also communicated regularly with her co-creators, acknowledging both their leadership and the difference they were making.

Throughout Project Front Line, Erin and her co-creators were guided by the belief that they could "be the difference." She said, "If you want to have an impact, that's possible. It starts within yourself, and then it's an external action and inviting others to participate in that. If you have an idea to help someone, just do it. . . . Whatever it is, no act of kindness is unworthy and doesn't go unrecognized."

Project Front Line succeeded in raising more than $50,000 from 542 local residents. Forty local establishments participated in preparing and delivering meals, and 8,130 frontline workers benefited from this meal service. Erin's example demonstrates that you don't need a centralized, national edict to make extraordinary things happen. One person can make a difference through her leadership and can raise the spirits and the well-being of an entire community.

Erin told us that the most important leadership lesson she learned was to "curate and conduct from your core values. Align your thoughts, words, and actions from a clear purpose and the results will be unprecedented. Who you speak with, who you collaborate with, and what you achieve stem from these shared principles. Everything you produce will resonate with those intentions."

Leaders like Erin understand that you have to comprehend fully the values, beliefs, and assumptions that drive you. No matter where you are in the organization, or what you are doing, you have to freely, and honestly, choose the principles that you will use to guide your actions. Before you can clearly communicate your message, you must be clear about the message you want to deliver. Before you can do what you say, you must be sure that you *mean* what you say. However, words themselves are not enough, no matter how noble. You must find *your* voice and authentically communicate your beliefs in actions that uniquely represent who you are so that others recognize that you are the one who's speaking and not someone else.

The most effective leaders are those who most frequently engage in the Model the Way leadership practice. Individuals asked their co-workers and colleagues to complete the LPI–Observer, indicating how often they observed that person engaging in the six leadership behaviors associated with Model the Way. Peers were also asked for an assessment of how effective they found this individual to be as a leader. The statistical analysis showed that effectiveness evaluations increased systematically as peers indicated this individual engaging more and more frequently in these leadership behaviors. The research evidence is clear. The place to begin your leadership journey, as Erin and other leaders experienced, is to clarify your values.

Clarify Your Values

Take a moment to think about a person in history whom you most admire—someone you could imagine following willingly. Who would this person be for you? - *Jesus Christ / King David / Regan*

Having asked this question of thousands of people around the globe, what stands out is that the historical leaders people admire most are individuals with strong beliefs about matters of principle. The leaders most often named all had an unwavering commitment to a clear set of values. They were all passionate about their causes. The lesson from this data is unmistakable: To become a leader people would willingly follow requires being a person of principle. Many people when reflecting on their Personal-Best Leadership Experiences echoed what Alan Spiegelman, wealth management advisor with a nationwide financial services company, realized: "Before you can be a leader of others, you need to know clearly who you are and what your core values are. Once you know that, then you can give your voice to those values and feel comfortable sharing them with others."

People expect their leaders to speak out on matters of values and conscience. Nevertheless, you cannot speak out if you do not know what is important to you, what you care about deeply. To speak effectively, you must find, as Alan reflected, "your authentic voice." Earning and sustaining personal credibility requires articulating your deeply held beliefs, as Brenda Aho, responsible for strategic planning for a regional distributing company, explained. She told us she expected her colleagues, and her six-year-old son, "to look to me as a leader and a role model." For her, this meant being authentic, and she said, "That comes from finding your own voice; by owning your values and being clear about who you are and what is most important to you. When we show up with authenticity, linking our actions with our espoused values and ideals, we earn the trust of our followers, who ultimately decide on our credibility as a leader."

As both Alan and Brenda point out, values are your guides, your personal bottom line. They supply you with a moral compass by which to navigate the course of your daily life. Clarity of values is essential to discerning which way is north, south, east, and west. The clearer you are about your values, the easier it is to stay on the path you have chosen. You especially need this kind of guidance in difficult and uncertain times. When there are daily challenges that can throw you off course, it is crucial that you have some signposts that tell you where you are and keep you on the right path.

Values also serve as guides to action. They inform your decisions about what to do and what not to do. They help you to know when to say yes, when to say no, and to understand *why* you made that choice. If, for instance, you believe that "heated debate" can stimulate thinking and creativity, then you should know what to do if people with differing views keep getting cut off when they offer up a fresh idea. If you value collaboration over individualistic achievement, then you will know what to do when your most experienced colleague skips team meetings and refuses to share information with others. If you value independence and initiative over conformity and obedience, you will be more likely to speak up and challenge a policy when you think it's wrong.

The LPI data reveals that the extent to which peers agree that their colleague is effective as a leader is dependent upon how they evaluate the clarity of that person's leadership philosophy. For those individuals perceived as most frequently clear about their leadership philosophy, their leadership effectiveness rating by their colleagues and co-workers is nearly twice that of individuals seen as rarely clear. The same pattern is repeated from the perspective of managers; that is, their managers agree that individuals who are most effective as leaders are definitely clear about their leadership philosophy.

Explore Your Inner Territory   The two of us were talking about where leadership begins, and our conversation went something like this:

Jim: I think leadership begins with discontent—when you are dissatisfied with the status quo and the ways things are currently going.

Barry: True enough, but that's too dismal a view for me. I think leadership actually begins with caring. What do you care enough about to
see if it could be any better?

Jim: Okay, then, let's look up the word "caring" in the dictionary.

We grabbed one off the shelf and opened it to *care*. The first meaning: "suffering of mind: GRIEF, SORROW." There it was. Suffering and
caring, discontent and concern, all come from the same source. When
there is something that we hold dear, we are willing to endure hardship to
secure and sustain it. The truest test of whether we care is whether we're
willing to suffer for it.

In time, we realized that what we were both saying is *that leadership
begins with something that grabs hold of you and won't let go.* There is
something that isn't working, and you care enough to do something
about it. Finding your voice requires exploring your inner territory to
discover what that "something" is. You have to take a journey into your
heart and soul to discover your values. You must wrestle with what is
inside of you long enough to determine what's really important to you,
what's underlying your choices and the boundaries and standards you
set, and what motivates you to take the actions you do.

John Robbins is the best-selling author of *Diet for a New America*,
and that book was the result of a ten-year odyssey and inner journey of
understanding and appreciating the links among nutrition, environmen-
talism, and animal rights. As John told us: "Make a statement with your
life that's consistent with your heart, that gives voice to what you really
feel is important. We don't have a lot of opportunities, most of us, to take
stands—that are seen anyway, that are visible. But my feeling is that you
take it, whether it's seen or not, whether it's recognized or not, whether
it's cheered or jeered. You do it because it's in you to do it, and because by
doing it you're being true to who you are."

You can only be authentic when you lead others according to the
values that matter most to you. Otherwise, you are just putting on an act.
If you do not care, how can you expect others to care? The fact is that the
first person who must follow you is you! To lead others, you first have to

believe in yourself. If you do not, others will not believe in you or have confidence in you, and consequently, will not willingly follow your lead. Sumaya Shakir, when at her leadership personal-best as part of a multinational information technology company, told us she had "to question myself about what I stood for, what was important to me, what approaches I was going to follow, what I was going to communicate, and what my expectations were. I had to know and believe first within myself. There were so many things that came into my mind all at once, but I had to focus on the core values I wanted to represent."

One of the overriding lessons to come out of the COVID-19 pandemic and the social unrest associated with the death of George Floyd was that challenges, hardships, and adversities caused people to come face-to-face with themselves. This was admittedly a rather harsh way of being reminded about what was most important and most valued. Values set the parameters for the hundreds of decisions that people made every day, consciously and subconsciously. People's performance and ability to handle stress most gracefully is directly related to the alignment between their values and actions. When faced with uncertainty, your values provide a compass, an internal magnetic north, which points you forward even when the path ahead is murky.

All of the most critical decisions you make involve values. For example, values determine how much emphasis to place on the immediate needs of the customer or the long-term interests of the company, how to apportion time between family and organizational responsibilities, or how soon you would gather together in large settings during the pandemic. When you are clear about your personal values, you are better prepared to make choices based on principle, rather than the whims, fashions, and pressures of the moment.

Discover Your Voice   To find your voice you have to discover what you care about, what defines you, and what makes you who you are. When Paul di Bari's operations section within the engineering services group took on the responsibility for the physical security of the healthcare system's 2.2 million-square-foot facility, he realized that this new assignment would require more detailed attention than had been paid in the past. He knew that he needed to be prepared "to clearly explain what my values were, my project management style and expectations" in meeting with various technicians and contractors. At the beginning of the project, Paul articulated his values and standards, establishing a baseline for performance and accountability. Because Paul was clear about his own values, he found it relatively easy to talk about them and subsequently to use them in setting standards and expectations.

Paul's experience illustrates that values serve as guides, and the clearer you and those around you are about values, the easier it is to commit to staying on the chosen path. With personal values clarity you are also better able to express yourself, so that everyone knows what you stand for. You have to give voice to these values, so that everyone knows that you are the one speaking. Novelist and nonfiction author Anne Lamott gives this advice to would-be writers in her classes, and it's also quite relevant for leaders:

> The truth of your experience can only come through in your own voice. If it is wrapped in someone else's voice, we readers are suspicious, as if you are dressed up in someone else's clothes. You cannot write out of someone else's big dark place; you can only write out of your own. Sometimes wearing someone else's style is very comforting, warm and pretty and bright, and it may loosen you up, tune you into the joys of language and rhythm and concern. But what you say will be an abstraction because it will not have sprung from direct experience; when you try to capture the truth of your experience in some other person's voice or on that person's terms, you are removing yourself one step further from what you have seen and what you know.[1]

You cannot lead through someone else's values, words, or experiences. Unless they're your values, words, and experiences, it's not the genuine you. And, if you are not the genuine article, can you really expect others to respect you? People do not follow your technique. They follow you—your message and your embodiment of that message. To be a leader, you must confront this central issue for yourself. You do not have to copy someone else, you don't have to read a script written by someone else, and you don't have to wear someone else's fashions. Instead, you are free to choose what you want to express and the way you want to express it. Researchers have consistently demonstrated a significant relationship between a leader's clarity and commitment to a set of core values and their likelihood of being successful.[2]

What can you do to be more conscious about the words you use, because words matter? They are as much a form of expression for leaders as they are for poets, singers, and writers. Words send signals. Is this an "argument" or a "disagreement"? When you say something is "hot," do you mean in temperature, spiciness, or relevance? Do you refer to your workplace as a war zone, barren desert, pressure cooker, or tropical island?

Parnav Sharma was volunteering with a nationwide organization that worked with fifth-graders in public schools that did not have creative arts programs. Frustrated by his seeming lack of progress with one student, he was losing his motivation, and not surprising, felt the same was true for the student he was mentoring. To re-energize himself, he told us how he had to remind himself about the reasons he had originally joined this organization and build a relationship with this student by talking to her about her interests and what she was looking for from him. Through this reflection, Parnav realized that to make an indelible impression on this student he needed to discover his own voice. "Finding my voice was not easy," Parnav explained, and in talking with this student he allowed her to guide the conversation. "It was difficult at first, but the enthusiasm in her eyes encouraged me to continue to establish my own voice and my own words. The result was a happy child," who at the end of a program gave him "a very creative thank-you card highlighting me as the best mentor she had had."

Clarity around values, as Parnav came to appreciate, goes a long way toward being able to express yourself and say what you want to say in a way that others immediately recognize as true to you. This experience is not unlike shopping for clothes. You can look in the window and see things that look good, but you'll want to try them on to see how they "fit" you before making a purchase. Otherwise, they'll remain in the closet because they don't make you feel comfortable, or feel like yourself, when you are with other people.

Build and Affirm Shared Values   Clarifying personal values is an essential step on your leadership journey. However, leaders do not just stand up for their own personal set of values. Authentic leaders also stand for the shared values of their collective constituents. In becoming an exemplary leader, you have to cross the chasm from "what *I* believe" to "what *we* believe." People are more loyal and committed when they believe that their values, your values, and those values of the organization are aligned. The quality and accuracy of communication and the integrity of the decision-making process increase when people feel that they have significant values in common with their colleagues. Which was precisely what Joyce Tan learned from her Personal-Best Leadership Experience, as part of a team that created a more streamlined process for contract execution at a global biopharmaceutical company. While her role involved being the legal operations analyst, she explained that because she and her "colleagues shared the same values and tried our best to abide by these principles, it made it easier to work together and accomplish our goals."

"Discovering and affirming shared values is the foundation for building productive and genuine work relationships. While honoring the diversity of those around you, you will still find that the foundation of relationships is built upon shared values. It's both unrealistic and unnecessary to get everyone to be in accord with everything. Moreover, to achieve it would negate the very advantages of inclusiveness. However, in moving forward, taking the first step, then a second, and then a third, people must have some common core of understanding. If disagreements over fundamental values continue, the result is intense conflict, false expectations, and diminished capacity.

Real estate agent Cathy Wang also has found that sharing her personal and work values creates a positive and productive climate for conversation. Clients, lenders, escrow officers, and other parties come to understand what her goals are and what they can expect when they work with her. "I have found that sharing my values is very powerful," she said, "because when my values align with what the clients believe, a foundation of mutual trust is created, and that results in a smoother process with demanding and sometimes tedious transactions."

Recognition of shared values provides a common language and framework for communicating how key decisions should be made. Research clearly shows that the alignment of individual, group, and institutional values generates tremendous energy.[3] Agreement intensifies commitment, enthusiasm, and drive. Individuals have reasons for caring about their work, and when people care about what they are doing, they are more effective and satisfied. They experience less stress and tension. Shared values also enable people to act both independently and interdependently.[4]

As Joyce's and Cathy's experiences demonstrate, you have to involve people in the process of identifying, clarifying, and reaching consensus on key values. A unified voice emerges from discovery and dialogue. You must provide a chance for the people you are working with to engage in a discussion of what the values mean, as well as how their personal beliefs and behaviors are both influenced by and aligned with them. Be prepared to discuss values and expectations in the recruitment, selection, and orientation of new people to your team, department, or program. Unity is forged, not forced.

Lead by Example

It is important that leaders forthrightly articulate the principles for which they stand and find alignment with the values of their colleagues and work team. But words are not sufficient. Leadership is values in action. Leaders *enact* the meaning of their personal and shared values in how they behave, in every decision they make, and in every step they take toward the future they envision. Leaders understand that they bring shared values to life in a variety of settings—in departmental meetings, one-on-one discussions, tweets, emails, social media, conversations over breaks and meals, and visits with suppliers, service providers, customers, clients, patrons, and the like. Statistically significant relationships were found in the LPI data between how often individuals are seen by their peers as setting a personal example of what they expect of others and the extent to which their colleagues felt valued by them and believed that they had the best interests of other people at heart.

When you lead by example—when your actions are consistent with your words and your espoused values—then people will consider you credible. In our research on leadership credibility, we asked people to answer the question, "So how does someone demonstrate credibility?" Tens of thousands of people from around the globe gave us essentially the same answer. Regardless of how they phrased it, the responses boiled down to this: "They do what they say they will do."

When it comes to deciding whether a leader is believable, people first listen to the words, and then they watch the actions. They listen to the talk, and then they watch the walk. They listen to the promises and then look for evidence that the commitments are kept. When words and deeds are congruent, the judgment handed down is "credible." The verdict when people do not see consistency is that you are, at best, unreliable, or, at worst, an outright hypocrite. "Credibility is the key to success," is what Joyce Tan learned in her personal-best experience: "If I say I am going to deliver something, then I must deliver, or I end up breaking the trust people have in me." The LPI data shows how dramatic the impact of frequently following through on promises and commitments is on assessments of leader effectiveness. As Figure 2 dramatically shows, 91 percent of peers strongly agree that the individuals who very frequently "do what they say they will do" are most effective as leaders. In comparison, less than 1 percent strongly agree for those individuals who only sometimes (or less) keep their promises and commitments.

There are significant signal-sending actions you can take to demonstrate that you live the shared values, that you take them seriously, and that you hold yourself and others accountable to them.[5] These include how you spend your time and what you pay attention to, how you handle critical incidents, the stories you tell, the language you use, the questions you ask, and how receptive you are to feedback.

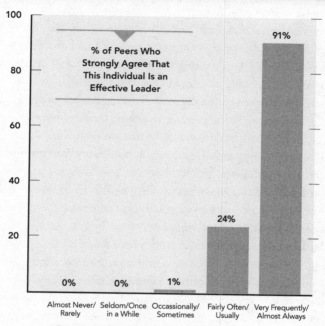

Figure 2 Only Those Individuals Who Keep Their Promises and Commitments Are Seen as Effective Leaders

Spend Your Time and Attention Wisely How you spend your time is the most precise indicator of what's important to you. What you spend your time paying attention to, working on, and with whom you spend it speak volumes to others about what your actual priorities are compared to what you might say you care about. Whatever your values are, they have to show up on your calendar if people are to believe that they are important.

While Greg Mills today is the CEO of a mobile game company, he continues to make use of the lessons from his Personal-Best Leadership Experience when he played high school water polo. He told us that although he was highly motivated to play, he had to keep reminding himself that it was a team sport: "I could set my own high standards, but I couldn't force my standards on other players." He wasn't the team's captain, but he decided to show his dedication by setting an example for his teammates. While each player was expected to be at every workout and to practice seriously, Greg led by example not only by being at every workout, but also by working out hard, usually being the last one to finish practice and leave the pool. As he explained, "If I told people to go to all the workouts, and I kept missing a few workouts a week, they wouldn't listen to me. Their confidence in me would diminish."

Setting an example often means doing exactly what Greg did—arriving early, staying late, working hard, and being there to show you care. It's about being the first to do something that everyone else should value. Whether the value is family, teamwork, hard work, or fun, the truest measure of what leaders deeply believe is how they spend their time. Constituents use it to judge whether a leader lives up to espoused standards. Visibly spending time on what is important shows that you are "putting your money where your mouth is."

Calendars never lie when it comes to sending a message to others about how you prioritize your time and how this allocation aligns with your values and priorities—or not. Time is a finite quantity, so you have to make sure the way you distribute your time is in sync with what you say is important and consistent with what you and your colleagues have agreed are priorities.

Turn Critical Incidents into Teachable Moments   Choosing to spend time on core values is essential in sending the signal that you are serious about them. Nevertheless, you cannot plan everything about your day. Even for the most disciplined leaders, the proverbial "stuff" happens. Chance occurrences—particularly at a time of stress and challenge—can become opportune moments to model and teach others around you valuable lessons about appropriate norms of behavior. Critical incidents offer leaders the chance to improvise while still staying true to the script. They cannot be planned. However, the way you handle these incidents— how you link actions and decisions to shared values—says volumes about what is imperative.

Jennifer Tran found out, for example, that being part of a team does not automatically mean that everyone has the same set of priorities. While working on a new technology project for a worldwide online payments company, which would have a huge impact on the way consumers paid for purchases, she discovered a problem with the documentation which would require further work. The team's copyeditor had already edited the documentation several times and was hesitant to step back and review it yet again. Jenn pushed back, reminding her teammate about the possibility of not creating a "great user experience"—a core shared value among all groups in their company. With that, the copyeditor reconsidered, and the team came up with a solution that satisfied everyone. "The fact that I stood up for this common value," Jenn told us, "was instrumental in both mitigating potential conflict and encouraging greater team spirit." For Jenn, this situation was not simply another problem to be dealt with; it was also a leadership opportunity moment to remind her colleagues about the importance of living up to their shared values.

Critical incidents are often the most dramatic sources of practical lessons about how people should and should not behave. Critical incidents provide you with the opportunity to put values squarely on the table so that you can reinforce the common ground for working together. By stepping up and confronting the situation, you make clear how shared values demand attention. You set an example for what it means to take actions based on values. By standing up for guiding principles under adverse circumstances, you demonstrate that shared values require a mutual commitment to align words and deeds. You also create teachable moments about how to solve problems and resolve disputes in ways that are consistent with shared values. Keep in mind, as Jennifer did, that the way you handle these incidents makes concrete what is most important to you and your colleagues.

Tell Stories to Reinforce Values and Connect with Actions   Stories are a powerful tool for calling attention to what's important and what's not, what works and what doesn't, what is and what could be.[6] Paul Smith, former director of consumer and communications research at Procter & Gamble and author of *Lead with a Story*, explains that the reason telling stories is so important is "because you can't just order people to 'be more creative' or to 'get motivated' or to 'start loving your job.' The human brain does not work that way. But you can lead them there with a good story." He points out that you cannot even successfully order people to "follow the rules" because nobody reads the rulebook. However, "people will read a good story about a guy who broke the rules and got fired, or a woman who followed the rules and got a raise. And that would be more effective than reading the rulebook anyway."[7]

In today's organizations, which seem obsessed with PowerPoint presentations, complex charts, and lengthy reports, storytelling may seem like a soft way of getting the hard stuff done. But the research shows something quite different. Consider the following. If you were trying to communicate the values of your organization, what would have more of an impact: a policy statement that reads, "Thou shalt provide timely services to our clients" or a story about how an individual from IT took up the challenge to go directly to the customer's site to work on a server problem? Similarly, what would be more persuasive: seeing statistics about how much stress criminal lawyers experience, or hearing a story about a local prosecutor who had committed suicide? Would you believe the words of a colleague more about the importance of making sure that online systems were always working if you had read it in a policy manual or heard stories about how that individual had come in on the weekend to ensure that the customer's service was up-and-running after a power outage?

If you answered "the story" in each of these instances, your answer is consistent with the data. In fact, information is more quickly and accurately remembered when it is first presented in the form of an example or story, especially compared to facts, figures, and formal policy pronouncements.[8] Stories are far better able to accomplish the objectives of teaching, mobilizing, and motivating than bullet points on a video, screen shares, poster boards, banners, slogans, policy announcements, and the like. Well-told stories reach inside people and pull them along.

Storytelling is an effective leadership practice because stories are generally simple, straightforward, timeless, and appeal to most everybody regardless of age, gender, or race. They are typically fun, a good method for empowering people by making them role models, and an effective way to pass along organizational traditions and reinforce key values. Stories serve as mental maps that help people make the connection between what is important—the purpose and values of their endeavor—and how to put these things into practice in a particular context. When people hear a story about how someone like themselves enacted a value, they are much more likely to see themselves doing the same.

Developing your skills in storytelling has another lasting benefit. It forces you to pay close attention to what is going on around you. When people hear you tell a story they are aware that you are paying attention, and when you relate a story about someone with whom they can identify, people are better able to envision acting similarly. Moreover, people seldom tire of hearing stories about themselves and the people they know. These are the stories repeated, and the lessons of these stories spread far and wide.

Watch Your Language   The words you use give voice to your mindset and beliefs. They also evoke images about what you aspire to create and how you expect people to behave. The words you choose have a powerful effect on how others see themselves and those around them, as well as the events you all share.

Researchers have documented the power of language in shaping thoughts and actions. Just a few words from someone can make the difference in the beliefs that people articulate. A publicized incident of hate mail sent to an African American student led to a study where researchers randomly stopped students walking across campus at that institution and asked them what they thought of the occurrence. Before the student could respond, a research partner impersonating another student would come up and answer with a response like "Well, he must have done something to deserve it." As you might expect, the first student's response was more often than not just like the student impersonator's response. The researchers then stopped another student and asked the same question, but this time the impersonator gave an alternative response, something like "There's no place for that kind of behavior on our campus." The student, questioned again, replicated the impersonator's response.[9]

This classic study dramatically illustrates how potent language is in influencing people's responses to what is going on around them. Language helps to build the frame around people's views of the world, so you need to be mindful of the words you choose. "Watch your language" takes on an entirely new meaning from the times your teacher scolded you in school for using an inappropriate word. Now it is about setting an example for others in how your language frames the context for thinking and talking about events and ideas and focuses attention on certain aspects of the subject. Just think about the impact of changing the expression from "I have to do this" to "I choose to do this." It's obvious that the latter puts you in the driver's seat and triggers your taking personal responsibility and accountability.

Consider, for example, the intriguing impact of language on people in experiments in which researchers told participants they were playing either the Community Game or the Wall Street Game.[10] In both scenarios, people played the same game by the same rules, with the only difference being that experimenters gave the game two different names. Of those playing the Community Game, 70 percent started out playing cooperatively and continued to do so throughout. Of those told they were playing the Wall Street Game, just the opposite occurred: 70 percent did not cooperate; and of the 30 percent who did cooperate, they stopped when they saw that others were not cooperating. Again, remember that the name, not the game itself, was the only thing that was different!

These experiments powerfully demonstrate why you must pay close attention to the language you use. You can influence people's behavior simply by giving the task or the team a name that evokes the kind of behavior implied by the name. If you want people to act like a community, use language that evokes a feeling of community. Want people to act like citizens of a village, then you have to talk about them that way, not as subordinates in a hierarchy. If you want people to appreciate the rich diversity in their organizations, you need to use inclusive language. If you want people to be creative, you have to use words that spark imagination, curiosity, exploration, and discovery. "Make it happen" was the mantra that Sophie Dean not only used in her Personal-Best Leadership Experience but for her marketing communication colleagues came to characterize how she approached challenging situations. One of her favorite expressions was: "I trust you to make it happen." Sophie felt that the success of their project was due to the "unity of our team and our trust in each other to *make it happen*."

Most people are "prisoners" of their organizational vocabulary.[11] If you disagree, try talking for a day about the people in an organization without using the words *employee, manager, boss, supervisor, staff, subordinate, rank-and-file,* or *hierarchy*. Sophie told us about another experience, early in her career, when she both worked for and volunteered a large amount of her time to help a close friend build her business from scratch. She was technically an employee for about 10 to 15 hours a week, but, Sophie explained, "I would often spend late nights and weekends on the phone or at her home hashing out details to build the business, improve processes, or develop new plans. That probably added up to thousands of hours of volunteer time, to help a friend. I was happy, even thrilled to be helping someone that I believed to be a dear friend. Her mission was my mission, and I was truly making a difference in her growth." This all changed one day when her friend referred to Sophie as her "staff." For Sophie this was as if a light bulb was switched on. "What am I doing," she wondered, "spending so much of my free time to help someone who only sees me as hired help and not a cherished friend? I was devastated. I quickly moved on to spending my time on other projects and felt completely unmotivated to continue to work for her. One word changed the entire dynamic of our relationship." Words can too easily trap you and others into a particular way of thinking about roles and relationships.

Language clearly communicates a message beyond the literal meaning of your words and phrases. In their book *Words Can Change Your Brain*, the authors show that "a single word has the power to influence the expression of genes that regulate physical and emotional stress."[12] Positive words strengthen areas in the frontal lobes, promoting the brain's cognitive functioning and building resiliency. Conversely, hostile language and angry words send alarm signals to the brain, as protection against any threats to survival, and partially shut down the logic and reasoning centers in the brain.

The language and words you use affect the way that you and others see and respond. They help frame the context for thinking and talking about events and ideas. In a similar way, the questions you ask and issues you raise force attention on the connections, or gaps, between espoused and enacted values.

Ask Purposeful Questions In your daily life, you probably ask a lot of questions. More than likely, most of them are intended to gather more information, get clarification, or reach a greater understanding of the information you received. From a leadership perspective, however, the questions you ask should do more than this. Well-phrased questions present opportunities to teach and reinforce shared values of the organization. Questions constitute one more measure of how serious you are about your espoused beliefs, and the substance of your questions reveals the values that warrant attention and the amount of energy that needs to be devoted to them.

The questions you ask should send people on journeys in their minds—journeys to explore what's important to you, the team, and the organization. The key to asking good leadership questions is to first think about the "quest" in your question: Where do you want to take this person (or group, unit, organization) with your question? What value or values are you trying to reinforce with your questions? What beliefs, perspectives, and principles do you want people to be thinking about?

Take a moment to think about the typical questions you ask in meetings, in one-on-ones, on phone calls, and during interviews. To what extent do they help to clarify and gain commitment to collective values? If they help only a little, then what can you ask that will increase commitment? What evidence do you want to ask for that will show that decisions are being made consistent with values? What questions can you ask if you want people to focus on integrity, or on trust, or on customer satisfaction, or on quality, innovation, growth, safety, or personal responsibility? What would you ask if the value were innovation? For example: What is the most creative idea you heard today? Or, What is the best suggestion you received from our customers today about how we can improve our products and services? If our competitors were going to put us out of business, what weakness of ours would they exploit?

You need to come up with a predictable set of questions that will help people to reflect on the core values and what they have done and can do each day to act on those values. In addition, the questions you ask ought to be ones that people will *expect* you to ask. They shouldn't be a surprise. Why? Because you want them to be thinking about these questions well before you ask them. You want people routinely to ask themselves these questions, knowing that you will be expecting an answer the next time you see them. It's been said that "leaders are present, even when they're absent." With so many people sheltered-in-place during the coronavirus pandemic and working remotely, one way that they stayed in touch with one another was by thinking about the questions that their colleagues and friends would be asking if they were together, face-to-face. In this same vein, before you take an action a simple ethics test is to ask yourself: "What would my mom or dad think about this decision?" It is because they are in your heart and mind, not because they are physically present that they continue to have impact on your thinking and choices.

In one way or another, the questions you ask are all a variation on a single theme: What are we doing to live out our values? The point is not to ask rhetorical questions (ones that have obvious answers or responses), but to get people to think about how their own actions are consistent with shared values. Your questions help to keep others focused and paying attention to what really matters.

There are additional benefits to asking questions. For one, they facilitate the development of the people you interact with, helping them escape the trap of their mental models. They broaden perspectives, expand response options, and promote taking responsibility for one's own viewpoints. Asking relevant questions also forces *you* to listen attentively to what people are saying and demonstrates that you respect their ideas and opinions. Moreover, if you are genuinely interested in what other people think, then you need to ask their opinion, especially before giving your own. Asking a simple question about what others think facilitates participation in decision making and increases support for the ultimate decision. Mark Linsky, who retired early from an engineering job with a high technology company, found a second career as a "super" volunteer (for example, with Rotary International, Junior Achievement, and AYSO—American Youth Soccer Organization). He told us how he learned that there was no such thing as a "stupid" question: "Often asking what may seem like a stupid question results in great learning. Don't worry about being seen as less than 100 percent knowledgeable about everything! When couched in a sense of uncertainty, such as 'I had thought . . .' or 'I was wondering why or if . . .' the opportunity to raise the bar on everyone's thinking is greatly increased."

Researchers have found that most people do not ask enough questions, and suggest that if you ask more questions, then your emotional intelligence will improve, which in turn will make you a better questioner.[13] Though not all questions are equally important, the ones that solicit more information have special power. Follow-up questions in a conversation signal that you "are listening, care, and want to know more. People interacting with a partner who asks lots of follow-up questions tend to feel respected and heard."[14]

Studies also show a robust and consistent relationship between question-asking and liking; people who ask more questions are better liked by their conversation partners. When people are instructed to ask more questions in their conversations, they are perceived as higher in responsiveness (an interpersonal construct that captures listening, understanding, validation, and care).[15] In these instances, follow-up questions were used more than any other type of question without people being explicitly told to ask them. A study of more than 500,000 business-to-business sales conversations (over the phone and via online platforms) showed a strong positive connection between the number of questions salespeople ask and their sales conversion rate.[16]

Finally, while seemingly counterintuitive, people perceive those who ask questions as both smarter and more interesting than those people who do not ask questions nor seek advice and input from others. It makes people feel good when you solicit their opinion and show respect for their competence. People also report that they generally seek advice from those who sought advice from them. Of course, you not only have to listen to their responses; you also must be open to giving their feedback serious consideration in subsequent decisions. Sincerity must underlie the asking.

Seek Feedback   How can you know that you are doing what you say—the *behavioral* definition of credibility—if you never receive feedback on your behavior? How can you be sure that your words and actions match if you do not get information about the extent to which others see them aligned? Feedback gives you a perspective about yourself that only others can see. With their insights, you have the opportunity to make improvements.

In reporting on his Personal-Best Leadership Experience, Alex Golkar shared how he learned this lesson. Initially, there was little alignment among his colleagues about the assignment of tasks and expected outcomes from their group's project, and he said there was lots of infighting, "with each of us being personally critical of each other." Alex told us that he "was forced to find my voice and act as an exemplar of the values that I wanted my groupmates to emulate." Once the team had worked through these issues and developed mutual respect, Alex asked his colleagues if they had any sort of feedback for him regarding his role in the project: "I realized that a good leader accepts feedback just as readily as he or she distributes it." Following his lead, team members turned to Alex and asked him for his opinions on how the group was progressing and what they could do to work even more productively together on the project. Whenever disagreements arose, Alex reported, "We established an informal system of feedback with one another to make sure we didn't revert back to unproductive arguments."

While Alex and his colleagues had positive experiences with giving and receiving feedback, the LPI data shows that asking for feedback is one of the *least* frequently engaged in leader behaviors. This is because the feedback process creates tension between two basic human needs: the need to learn and grow and the need to be accepted just the way we are.[17] Even what seems like a mild, gentle, or relatively harmless suggestion can leave you feeling angry, anxious, or threatened. Another reason why most people are not proactive in seeking feedback is their fear of feeling exposed—exposed as not being perfect, as not knowing everything, as not being fully up to the task.

In spite of these emotional and mental strains, there is simply no way to get around the fact that while you might not always like the feedback you receive, it is the only way you can really know how you are doing and possibly learn ways you can become even better. The good news is that researchers have found that people who seek out disconfirming feedback (that is, feedback contrary to their self-perceptions) perform better than those who only listen to people who see their positive qualities. "Being aware of your weaknesses and shortcomings," they say, "whether you like it or not, is critical to improvement."[18] Mark Linsky told us that, both as an engineer and in his various volunteer roles, he always thought of feedback as gift. "Like any gift," he said, "you can choose what you do with it: Keep it, throw it away, or use it at some later time, and so on. And, like a gift, you should assume that feedback has been given with the intent that it is something you would want."

Self-reflection, the willingness to seek feedback, and the ability to engage in new behaviors based on this information is predictive of future success in managerial jobs.[19] You can't learn very much if you are unwilling to find out more about the impact of your behavior on the performance of those around you. Self-awareness is an essential ingredient in personal happiness as well as professional success. Without it, you can move through relationships and experiences disconnected with how others receive and perceive you, and often be clueless about why you are not having the positive impact you expected.

It is also true that most people are not used to providing feedback, even when it's solicited. But unless you ask, people are unlikely to tell you what they think. You invite feedback; you cannot demand it. Researchers have found, however, that feedback is often too vague to be helpful, failing to highlight what you should do to improve (which presumably is the reason for seeking feedback in the first place). The solution? Ask for advice. For example, instead of asking, "How well did I do in that meeting?" you might say, "One thing I am trying to get better at is encouraging others to contribute ideas. I tried to do that during our meeting today. How do you think it went? What could I have done differently?" In a series of experiments, researchers found that "people received more effective input when they asked for advice rather than feedback."[20] Compared to those asked to give feedback, those asked to provide advice suggested 34 percent more areas for improvement and 56 percent more ways to improve. Feedback is too often associated with "being evaluated" and attends to what has already happened. When asked to provide "advice," people focus less on evaluation and more on offering suggestions about possible future actions

You will also find that the more frequently feedback becomes part of everyday conversations, the easier it will be to hear and deal with it as constructive, especially when everyone involved shares similar values and aspirations. The point is not to affix blame but to exercise curiosity about what happened and "what can be learned?" so that any problems, mistakes, misunderstandings, and the like that may have occurred are not repeated. Keep in mind, however, that if you do not do anything with the feedback you receive, people will stop giving it to you. They are liable to believe that you are arrogant enough to think that you are smarter than everyone else is or that you do not care about what anyone else has to say. Either of these outcomes seriously undermines your credibility and effectiveness as a leader. Finally, a side benefit of making it easy for people to give you feedback is that your example increases the likelihood that people will accept honest feedback from you. Of course, you must be sincere in your desire to improve and demonstrate that you are open to knowing how others see you.

Take Action to Model the Way

The first step you must take along the path to becoming an exemplary leader is inward, toward discovering and owning your personal values and beliefs. In finding your voice, you will discern the principles that you want to guide your decisions and actions and you develop the capacity to express "who you are" in unique ways. And yet, leadership is not merely about your values. Just as your values drive your commitment, your constituents' values drive theirs. Successfully leading others requires an understanding and affirmation of shared values—the principles that can galvanize and strengthen collective commitment.

Setting the example is how you demonstrate that you mean what you say—and that the organization means what it says. Leading by example is how you make visions and values tangible. Walking the talk, doing what you say, and being consistent in word and deed is how you and your team build credibility and is the ultimate test of whether or not people will believe what you say. You earn that credibility on a moment-by-moment, action-by-action basis. How you spend your time, what you pay attention to, the way you deal with critical incidents, the stories you tell, the language you use, the questions you ask, and how receptive you are to feedback are actions that provide evidence that you are "the real deal" and worthy of being listened to and followed by others.

In the next chapter we explain how you can create meaning and purpose in the longer term. We'll explore how you Inspire a Shared Vision by envisioning the future and enlisting others.

Here are two recommended actions that you should take to continuously strengthen your competence in the leadership practice of Model the Way:

Clarify Values. Although you may have thought about your values and how you define leadership, you may still be working to concisely articulate your leadership philosophy and talk about the values that are important to you. Keep in mind that leadership is a journey, not a destination—and that as you experience new situations, take in new information, and grow in confidence as a leader, your philosophy of leadership is likely to change and mature as well. Reflect and revisit your leadership values and beliefs at regular intervals by asking yourself what leadership challenges you've experienced or observed recently, how they've impacted your ideas about leadership as a practice, and how your goals as a leader might have changed as a result. Don't let your philosophy of leadership become static. Make sure it stays relevant to who you are and what you're actually doing.

Set an Example. No matter what you say or how you ask others to behave, your *own* actions will always serve as the truest indicator of your priorities and standards. You have to walk the talk. Before asking something of someone else, ask yourself: Would I be, or have I been, willing to do this? Continually evaluate whether or not your values are aligned with your expectations and your actions. At the end of each day, ask yourself these three questions:

> What have I done today that demonstrated my personal commitment to our shared values?

> What have I done today that might have, even inadvertently, demonstrated a lack of commitment?

> What can I do tomorrow to make sure I set a good example?

Ask a trusted colleague for feedback on your answers to these questions in order to provide validation that you are doing what you say you will do.

CHAPTER 3

Inspire a Shared Vision

IT WAS LATE one evening when Diann Grimm experienced a perplexing "aha moment!"—"I am living someone else's dream!" Having recently retired from a long career in public education, Diann was working as a curriculum developer for an early childhood education publisher. She brought a lot to the job, and though the work was important, it didn't feel personally meaningful. So she asked herself a poignant question: "What is *my* dream?" Wrestling inside herself to find an answer would set her on a new path: "I want to continue to foster education and learning, but to do so in an innovative way." But how was she going to make this dream a reality?

Over the years on her summer breaks, Diann had participated in many volunteer projects, most of them centered on early childhood education in developing countries. She felt especially called to Nepal, where she'd spent a summer working with Bhupendra (Bhupi) Ghimire, the executive director of Volunteers Initiative Nepal (VIN). Diann decided to reach out to her old friend to see if her aspirations and his might come together in ways that would be meaningful to both of them.

Her timing was serendipitous, as Bhupi was planning to bring VIN to Nepal's Okhaldhunga district, where he himself had grown up. This underdeveloped area is far from tourist trails, and its residents, who depend on subsistence farming and bartering, had minimal infrastructure for education or any other public services. Within two weeks of Bhupi asking her, "Why don't you come to Nepal and help us do this?" Diann flew there, ready to make the most of this opportunity and eager to enact her and Bhupi's visions of a better future for Nepali children.

In Nepal, children begin school at age six, which means they often miss out on education during a crucial time in their development. By extension, older children, typically girls, are also unable to take advantage of educational opportunities, as they are often made to stay home and care for their younger siblings. Because of her long-term experience, it was decided that Diann would take the lead on the early childhood education piece of the larger VIN program. This would allow VIN to make "the best use of my passion and past experiences," she told us.

While the residents and local government were enthusiastic about the preschool idea, they were skeptical about how it could actually happen. Rather than Bhupi and Diann coming in to impose their vision, everyone in the community had to be involved and enlisted because the preschool would have great significance beyond itself. For example, it would make it possible for older siblings to start attending school. It also presented an opportunity for some of the district's women to make money outside of the home or to contribute to the community, as they would be the ones who would actually teach and volunteer in the schools. According to Diann, "This would be a true partnership among all parties, and one that created a shared sense of purpose among the community." Their combined efforts since Diann first returned to Nepal led to the establishment of 48 classrooms in a number of Nepal's villages and districts, providing early childhood education to an average of 900 children per year. Her alliance with Bhupi and VIN also inspired Diann to establish her own nonprofit organization, Partners in Sustainable Learning, which builds schools, develops curriculum, trains teachers, and provides classrooms with sustainable supplies.

Diann's vision has been realized in ways she never thought possible. "I had no idea where this would take me when I started," she said, "but

I had a big dream and I just couldn't get it out of my head. Every set-back was just a temporary obstacle to making it all happen. The reward is in the faces of the children and their parents, and in the realization that while I may never know these kids as adults, they will have a better chance to thrive as a result of our efforts." She also realized that her dream became a reality as a result of aligning with the hopes and aspirations of Bhupi, VIN, and the scores of teachers and villagers she works with.[1]

The leaders we studied share with Diann the perspective that bringing meaning to life in the present by focusing on making life better in the future is essential to making extraordinary things happen. Leaders dream of what might be. Everyone at some time in their lives has had a glimpse of the future. You know, that time when you imagined running your own business, or that dream of traveling to an exotic place, or that bold idea for a game-changing new product, or that burning desire to get an advanced degree. It might have been that sense of purpose you felt when you signed up for the sustainability campaign, or that calling to join a cause and make this a better planet, or that uplifting sense you got when picturing kids playing without fear in a neighborhood. Leaders take these dreams seriously and act to make them a reality.

We discovered in our research that people *expect* leaders to be forward-looking. They want leaders to describe not simply the present reality; they want them to talk about the desired outcomes—what can be, not just what is. The capacity to imagine and articulate exciting future possibilities is one of the defining competences of leaders. While being forward-looking and visionary is not necessarily something people expect of a colleague, you need to take your internal magnetic north and focus it on the exciting possibilities that surround you and every project.

In the exercise of leadership, you have to be able to imagine a positive future and to give the work that is being done a sense of meaning and purpose.[2] All enterprises or projects, big or small, originate in the mind's eye; they begin with imagination and with the belief that what's now only an image can one day be made real. When you envision the future you want for yourself and others, and when you feel passionate about the legacy you want to leave, you are much more likely to take that first step forward.

But just like Diann, it's not just about your vision. It's really about creating a *shared* vision. When visions are shared, they attract more people, sustain higher levels of motivation, and withstand more challenges than those that are singular. You have to make sure that what you can see is also something that others can see.

The most effective leaders are those who most frequently engage in the Inspire a Shared Vision leadership practice. Individuals asked their colleagues to complete the LPI–Observer, indicating how often they observed that person engaging in the six leadership behaviors associated with Inspire a Shared Vision. Peers were also asked for an assessment of how effective they found this individual to be as a leader. The statistical analysis showed that effectiveness evaluations increased systematically as peers indicated this individual engaging more and more frequently in these leadership behaviors.

Clarify Your Vision

No matter what you call it—*vision, purpose, mission, legacy, dream, calling,* or *burning agenda*—the intent is the same. There is something greater than present rewards that infuses life and work with meaning and importance—something that transcends the here-and-now and draws people forward.

People who exercise leadership are propelled by that sense of purpose, mission, and vision. They want to accomplish something that no one else has yet achieved. What that something is comes from within. That's why, just as we said about values, you must first clarify your own vision of the future before you can expect to enlist others in a shared vision. Before you can inspire others, you have to inspire yourself.

Crossing the chasm from individual contributor to leader requires fully embracing the need to develop the capacity to envision the future. Making the transition from average to exemplary leader, regardless of level, requires the dedication to master it. And how does a new leader develop the capacity to be forward-looking? The answer is deceptively simple: Spend more time in the future. You have to carve out more time each week to peering into the distance and imagining what might be out there. You have to spend the time today in order to have the time tomorrow.

In this digital age, however, you might wonder: "How can I have a vision of what's going to happen five or ten or even two years from now, when I don't even know what's going to happen next week or even over these next few months?" There are a couple of ways of answering this question. First, not knowing exactly what is going to happen five or ten years from now doesn't stop parents from saving for college for their kids, or young workers from investing in 401Ks for their eventual retirement, or entrepreneurs from working in their apartments inventing a break-through product that won't be marketable for years, or youth activists from speaking up about the need for a sustainable environment. Just because you can't predict the future doesn't mean you should not imagine a better one. These are all forward-looking acts that are undeterred by the uncertainties of the present.

Another way to think about the importance of envisioning the future is to imagine you're driving along the Pacific Coast Highway heading south from San Francisco on a bright, sunny day. The hills are on your left; the ocean, on your right. On some curves, the cliffs plunge several hundred feet to the water. You can see for miles and miles. You're cruising along at the speed limit, tunes blaring, top down, wind in your hair, and not a care in the world. Suddenly, without warning, you come around a bend in the road, and there's a thick blanket of fog covering the road and you can't see beyond the hood of your car. What do you do? We've asked this question many, many times and we get the same answers: "I slow way down, turn my lights on, turn the music off, grab the steering wheel with both hands, tense up, and even lean forward." Then you go around the next curve in the road, where the fog has lifted, and it's clear again. What do you do now? You relax, accelerate, turn the lights off, turn the music back on, and enjoy the scenery.

This analogy illustrates the importance of clarity of vision, *especially* what it takes to move ahead quickly and confidently. How fast can you drive in the fog without risking your own or other people's lives? How comfortable are you riding in a car with someone else who drives fast in the fog? Are you able to drive more quickly when it's foggy or when it's clear? It's obvious, isn't it? "You can go more quickly when your vision is clear," is precisely what Kyle Harvey found out when he had to coordinate with a colleague to complete a marketing video project. They got off to a slow start, and how they were supposed to work together was confusing. Knowing that his colleague was extremely creative and artistic, Kyle took the initiative to share some possible approaches and asked for her ideas and thoughts about how this project could incorporate her talents and interests. "That's all it took," he told us. "The fog analogy was especially strong in this instance. When our vision was unclear, we pulled off to the side of the road and did not continue to drive." However, after finding clarity, "We were back on the road and moving past the fog."

Discover Your Theme Just knowing that having a vision is essential doesn't make one pop out of your head like a bright light bulb. When we ask people to tell us where their visions come from, they often have great difficulty describing the process. And when they do provide an answer, typically it's more about a feeling, a sense, a gut reaction, a hunch. After all, there's no map, or interstate highway, to the future. When people first begin to exercise leadership they typically don't have a *clear* vision of the future.

What they do have—and what you, too, have—are concerns, desires, principles, hypotheses, propositions, arguments, hopes, and dreams— core concepts around which you organize your aspirations and actions. Visions are projections of your fundamental beliefs and assumptions about human nature, technology, economics, science, politics, art, ethics, and the like. Leaders often begin the process of envisioning the future by discovering the "theme" that ties together these inner whisperings, much like composers find a musical theme from all the notes that swirl in their minds. Your central theme in life more than likely wasn't something that just occurred to you this morning. It's been there for a long time. You may not have ever explored your past for a persistent and repeating ideal, but if you were to examine the recurring theme in your life, what might you find?

Megan Davidson, responsible for communications and data strategy at a global Internet company, described the feedback she received from her colleagues on the *Leadership Practices Inventory* as "particularly poignant because as an individual contributor most of my projects require frequent collaboration with co-workers. Improving my ability to Inspire a Shared Vision among co-workers would directly impact the success of my projects." The first action she took was to identify her own vision for the future for the projects she was leading within her multinational technology company by reflecting on her past. Since graduating college, Megan had held a new position in a different industry every two to three years. She had been a seventh-grade math teacher, managed clients ranging from nonprofit to engineering professionals, and worked at both startups and large companies more than 100 years old. The common thread among these diverse experiences, she realized, was "my fierce belief in the value of a 'customer focus.' I love improving the experience of students, users, customers, and the like, and I have sought out job opportunities that allow me to do so."

What leaders, just like Megan, eventually say about their vision is that it is an elaboration, interpretation, and variation on a "common thread" or theme. So what are your fundamental beliefs and assumptions about life and work that keep recurring in your life? What are the themes that keep repeating themselves? What are the causes you contribute to, the things that keep you up at night, and the "I wish" that you find yourself repeating?

Finding your vision, like finding your voice, is a process of self-exploration and self-creation. It's an intuitive, emotional process. What we've seen is that exemplary leaders have a passion for their projects, their causes, their programs, their subject matter, their technologies, their communities, their families—something other than their own fame and fortune. Your inner passion is an indicator of what you feel mostly deeply about and find worthwhile in and of itself. It's a clue to what is *intrinsically* rewarding to you. Leaders care about something much bigger than themselves. They care about making a difference, changing the status quo in some meaningful way. What do you care about most deeply? What do you wish for most often?

If you don't care deeply for and about something, then how can you expect others to feel any sense of conviction? How can you expect others to get jazzed if you're not energized and excited? How can you expect others to suffer through the inevitable long hours and hard work if you're not similarly inclined? Emotions are contagious, and when you express your passion, others are more likely to be infected by it than if you keep it to yourself.

Explore Your Past　As contradictory as it might seem, in aiming for the future you need to look back into your past, as Megan Davidson did. Looking backward can actually enable you to see farther than if you only stare straight ahead. Understanding your personal history can help you identify themes, patterns, and beliefs that both underscore why you care about particular issues or circumstances now and explain why making them better in the future is such a high priority.

People have told us how reflecting and analyzing their Personal-Best Leadership Experiences was enlightening for them. By highlighting critical lessons from the past, they were able to generate insightful roadmaps for leadership highways still to be explored. The knowledge gained from direct experience and active searching, once stored in the subconscious, becomes the basis for leaders' intuition, insight, and vision.

Nicklaus Danialy, a graduate student about ready to find his first full-time job, told us how he had "a very hazy idea of what I want for the future, and so I asked myself what it is I want to achieve in the future, because without a clear end in mind everything else is irrelevant. I looked back throughout my life and thought about the principles I adhere to most diligently, and used these as the starting point for clarifying my vision." The path that William Hwang followed was similar. His passion was ignited when he reflected upon his own experiences in high school, where several special summer programs he had attended "born from someone's imagination and hard work . . . changed, reshaped, and influenced me in amazing ways. They helped me focus, opened my eyes to new and exciting possibilities." He remembered a track teammate who had few role models and was on probation throughout high school. Thinking about him sparked, as William explained, "a burning desire to

do something to help others who might be lacking the same opportunities he had had." He decided to devote himself to children who needed it
most, and the nonprofit InnoWorks Academy was born.

As both Nick and William learned to appreciate, when you look first
into your past, you elongate your future. You also enrich your future and
give it detail as you recall the richness of your past experiences. To be able
to envision the possibilities in the distant future, look back into your life.
When you do, you're likely to find that your central theme has been there
for a long time.

In addition to identifying lifelong themes, there's another benefit to
looking back before looking ahead. You gain a greater appreciation for
how long it can take to fulfill aspirations, and see that the path to the
future is not a straight line. Just as in sailing, because you can't control
everything around you (such as the winds and the currents), you have to
tack, zigging back and forth as you make your way forward. No doubt
there will be ups and downs for you in any worthwhile pursuit, and
you'll veer into territory that you haven't traversed before, which is all
the more reason why you need to have a firm picture in your mind of
where you are going and why it is important to get there. Furthermore,
you may also realize in the journey that there may be new summits that
you want to climb.

None of this is to say that the past *is* your future. Adopting that
extremely dangerous perspective would be like trying to drive to the
future while looking only in the rearview mirror. With that point of view,
you'd drive you and your colleagues right off a cliff. Avail yourself of the
richest set of experiences possible. As you broaden your experiences and
expand your network of connections, your time horizons will also
stretch forward.

Immerse Yourself   As you acquire experience, you naturally
acquire information about what happens, how things happen, and
who makes things happen in your team, project, or organization, in a
profession, on a campus, or within an industry, community, or family.
When you're presented with an unfamiliar problem, you consciously (or
unconsciously) draw upon your experiences to help solve it. You select

crucial information, make relevant comparisons, and integrate lessons you've learned with the current situation. For the experienced leader, all of this may happen in a matter of seconds. But it's the years of direct contact with a variety of problems and situations that equips that individual with unique insight. It is through listening, reading, feeling, and sensing that leaders improve their visions. They develop an intuitive sense for what is going to happen down the road—they can anticipate what is just around the corner up ahead (i.e., the future). They are also sufficiently self-aware to recognize their biases because having experience and expertise can also blind you to new, important information. Exemplary leaders take care to look beyond the data that confirms their initial judgments.

To develop this same capacity, you need to immerse yourself in the present. You have to get off automatic pilot, believing that you know everything you need to know, viewing the world through pre-established categories, and not noticing what's going on around you. To increase your ability to conceive of new and creative solutions to today's problems, you have to be present in the present. You have to stop, look, and listen. It's only when you understand the current challenges that you will be able to imagine a better tomorrow.

Set aside some time each day to stop doing "stuff." Create some white space on your calendar. Remind yourself that your electronic devices have an off switch. Stop being in motion. Then start noticing more of what's going on around you right now.

Look around your workplace and community. What are people doing they didn't do a few years ago? What are people wearing, using, and discarding? How are people interacting? How do workplaces and communities look, and feel different, now compared to how they once did? What are the current trends popular these days? Why?

Listen to those around you. What are their hot topics of conversation? What are they saying they need and want? What are they saying that gets in the way of them doing their best? What do they think should be changed? Listen as well to the weak signals; take note of what's not being said. Listen for things you've never heard before. What does all this tell you about where things are going? What's it telling you about what lies just around the corner?

Consider again Megan Davidson's experience. As she was participating on a few project teams, she began to see that there were competing priorities, unclear roles and responsibilities, and communication pathways that had created inconsistencies. Her initial hypothesis was that some of the technology tools had been created without a clearly defined strategy and "joining other teams' meetings gave me insight into why recent tools had been created and I started to realize that the new tools had created silos of information, which created new challenges." Because she was able to listen and look around, Megan was able to "see" that the problem was less the number of tools in play and more about the lack of clearly defined relationships among them.

Envisioning the future is a process that begins with an inspiration, a feeling, or a sense that something is worth doing. Your vision of the future may be fuzzy, but at least you're focused on a meaningful theme. You believe that the present situation could be better than it is today. You act on your instincts, and the vision gets a little clearer. You do something else that moves you forward, and the vision gets a little clearer still. You pay attention to it, experience it, immerse yourself in it. You start the process, and over time you see more detail in your dream. It's an iterative process, one that eventually results in something that you and others can articulate, and literally see.

Get Others on Board

Leadership requires more than just having a vision, painting a picture of it, and selling your personal view of the world. You need to imagine the end result and be able to communicate your vision of the future such that your constituents can see their own ideals and aspirations incorporated and appreciated. They want to see themselves in the future that you are envisioning, and this requires getting others on board who have to help implement the vision. People don't want to be told what to do or where to go, no matter how right it might be; they want to be part of the vision development process.

Visions are about hopes, dreams, and aspirations. They're declarations of a strong desire to achieve something ambitious. They're expressions of optimism. Can you imagine being able to enlist others in a cause by saying, "I'd like you to join me in doing the ordinary?" Not likely. Visions stretch people to imagine exciting possibilities, breakthrough programs, or revolutionary social change. However, grand aspirations such as these cannot be achieved until they are also shared by others you want to enlist.

Kim-Ha Ho, senior accountant within the business services organization at a major university, works with multiple teams across many disciplines. She assumed that vision was, in her words, "not what I need to worry about because my role is so far removed from the vision of the top people. Vision is neither my responsibility, nor expected of me." However, when reflecting on this more, she realized that she had many conversations and opportunities to look holistically for ways to see how "my own vision would fit within that of the team, the unit, the department." Her department's vision was "to support all operations . . . by providing total financial services. We will be your partners to help campus departments solve their financial challenges and assist in your financial planning needs." Moving away from a very transactional perspective, she envisioned how she could be more transformational by coaching and sharing knowledge: "I proactively make it a shared vision that campus departments have the tools and skills they need to independently and sustainably make their own subjective financial decisions." Enlisting in a common vision helps, Kim explains, because "my constituents, my team, and myself look inward to acknowledge our long-term interests in well-run and self-sustained operations."

You can't impose a vision on others. It has to be something that has meaning to them, not just to you. Leaders must foster conditions under which people will do things because they want to, not because they have to. Leaders create environments where team, department, program, or institutional visions and personal values intersect. A strong correlation was found in the LPI data between the frequency to which peers reported that their colleague showed people "how their long-term interests can be realized by enlisting in a common vision" and the extent to which they would recommend this person to others as a good leader. People also expressed a stronger sense of team spirit within their group the more that they indicated this individual was able to paint a "big picture" about what they aspired to accomplish.

It's not enough for you to be clear about your vision and values; you must be attentive to those around you. Ask yourself who else must understand, accept, and commit to the vision. If you can't find alignment between what you care about and what others care about, then you won't find a common purpose or achieve much success in changing the status quo.

When people shared with us their Personal-Best Leadership Experiences, they frequently talked about the need to gain buy-in from others on the vision. They explained how they had to communicate the purpose and build support for a unified direction. They knew that everyone had to commit to a common purpose. They understood that to get everyone on the same journey, they had to be able to communicate *why* others should want to join in, what it would mean to them, and how it would benefit them. While you might be able to see how others' needs and interests are served, if they can't also see how their needs are connected to the larger vision, they will be reluctant to climb aboard. But when they do, the team's ability to change and reach its potential soars.

Inspiring others to keep up the hard work is seldom easy, especially when you are trying to apply this leadership practice with your children. However, consider this experience that Amy Tomlinson shared with us as an example of how she was applying these leadership concepts in her personal life:

> I laid out intentions to incorporate the idea of inviting someone to the leadership table to peek behind the curtain, get a first-hand experience, ask questions, and interact with our team's shared vision. Putting this into action happened in a place one might least expect, in this instance with our eight-year-old son.

We gave him a peek behind the curtain. Our son wanted more relaxed rules around using electronics on the weekends. As parents, we had set the rules but never took the time to share the meaning or purpose. Once we took the time to paint the big picture and describe a compelling image of what the future could look like, we were able to reach a shared understanding and buy-in. We then incorporated his aspirations and dream of the future to adjust our family rules. The change has been remarkable. We now have an eight-year-old boy working to demonstrate responsible choices and behaviors throughout his day, in order to earn further independence with his electronic devices.

This shared vision, says Amy, "has put our family on the same page working toward a common goal. It's amazing how much more children can process and understand when given the opportunity." The same is certainly true for adults, as well!

Listen Deeply Getting others on board means that you need to listen deeply to others. You have to engage the people you are involved with and work with in conversations about their lives, about their own hopes and dreams, and how they can see these realized by sharing and participating in the vision. Creating a common vision is about developing a *shared* sense of destiny. It's about enrolling others so that they can *see* how their own interests and aspirations are aligned with the vision and can thereby become mobilized to commit their individual energies to its realization.

For Amanda Itilong her position as a Patient Advocate on the American College of Radiology's Patient and Family Care Commission started with a tweet about the frustrations she faced visiting her radiologist's office. Living with cancer for more than a decade means that Amanda has had a lot of scans. She often sees the same problems over and over again on each visit, and she also sees many sharable best practices on her visits. The more Amanda listened and engaged with radiologists, the more they were open to listening to her. After all, both sides shared the same aspiration to make undergoing exams "quick and easy." Her patient-centered approach resonated with radiologists who wanted to reduce "scanxiety," and they realized that to do so would require listening very deeply to their patients, like Amanda, who were the only ones who can describe the true experience of radiology from the other side. As a patient advocate she had no formal power in the system, but she was able to enlist others in a common vision by appealing to shared aspirations. Getting others on board was as simple as telling her story in a way that walked the radiologists through each step that a patient experiences in the process of getting a scan. Discovering common aspirations are required steps that every leader must take in enlisting others. No matter how grand the dream of an individual visionary, or the frustrations of an individual patient like Amanda, if others don't see in it the possibility of realizing their own hopes and desires, they won't follow. You must show others how they, too, will be served by the long-term vision of the future, how their specific needs can be satisfied. That takes attentive listening.

To sense the purpose in others requires understanding people at a much deeper level than you may normally find comfortable. It requires exploring their strongest yearnings and their deepest fears. It means developing a profound awareness of their joys and sorrows. It demands understanding life as they experience it. It is by getting to know your constituents, by listening to them, and by soliciting their advice that you become better able to give voice to their feelings. You can then stand before others and say with assurance, "Here's what I heard you say that you want for yourselves. Here's how your needs and interests will be served by enlisting in a common cause." In a sense, you hold up a mirror and reflect back to your constituents what they say they most desire. When people see that reflection, they recognize themselves and can embrace the image.

Appreciating that leadership is a relationship puts listening in its proper perspective. It has been said that no great idea enters the mind through an open mouth, so you can't expect to have all the ideas or all of the answers yourself. People want to be listened to, and they are genuinely motivated in making sure that you understand, appreciate, and are incorporating their hopes and dreams. Find the time to listen by getting out of your cubicle, up from your desk or machine, and wandering into other people's workplaces. Have coffee, breakfast, lunch, afternoon breaks, or some unstructured occasion to be with people and find out what's going on with them. If you're working remotely, make sure to take the time to just listen in virtual meetings. Not every call or digital meeting needs to be full of structured presentations or shared screens to give reports with charts and slides. Spend some time building relationships, even in virtual settings, and avoid being 100 percent task-driven (it's exhausting). Be creative by asking people to play their favorite songs from their music library or showing some photos from their gardens or recent trips. Attending with your eyes can often be more powerful than simply attending with your ears.

What do you do if people can't articulate what they want? What if people don't know what they need? This is even more reason to listen deeply. Listening is not just about the words; it's about paying attention and reading between the lines, taking note of what's unspoken, noticing what makes them smile, what gets them angry, how they spend their time, and so on. From a leadership perspective you can be sure that everyone wants a tomorrow that is better than today, and while they don't all want the same thing, they do all want the future to be an improvement. What would that improvement look like?

Discover a Common Purpose   Have you ever asked others on your team, program, or department why they stay? Take a moment to think about the vast majority of those who stay, and ask why they stick around. Think about why you do. The most important reason people give about why they don't leave or aren't looking around for another position is that they find the work they are doing or the service they are providing to be challenging, meaningful, and purposeful. And researchers have reported that people who are purpose-oriented are more satisfied with their jobs than those who are not.[3] People want a chance to be tested; a chance to make it on their own; a chance to take part in a social experiment; a chance to do something well; a chance to do something good; a chance to change the way things are. Aren't these the essence of what most leadership opportunities are all about?

What people want from their workplace has not changed very dramatically over the years despite economic upturns and downturns. Regardless of profession, industry, or location, people rank the importance of "interesting work" well above "high income." And the quality of leadership ("working for a leader with vision and values") is even more motivating than dollars. Would it surprise you that the most frequently mentioned measure of success in work life is "personal satisfaction for doing a good job"? People cite this between three and four times as often as "getting ahead" or "making a good living."[4] One of the crucial realizations people have from reflecting on their Personal-Best Leadership Experiences is that once team members have a sense of purpose and are all on the same page, then everyone feels both responsible and motivated to make a difference.

There is a deep human yearning to make a difference. People want to know that they're doing something meaningful on this earth, that there's a purpose to their existence. Work can provide that purpose, and increasingly the workplace is where people pursue meaning and identity.[5] The best teams and workplaces are able to bring out and make use of this human longing by communicating the meaning and significance of what's being done so that people understand their own important role in creating it.

When you can clearly communicate a shared vision of an organization, you ennoble those who work on its behalf. You elevate the human spirit. While you can't impose your vision of the future on others, you can liberate the visions that are already stirring inside of people. When you communicate a shared vision you are awakening and arousing the belief that people can achieve something grand and unique. What truly pulls people forward, especially in more challenging and volatile times, is the exciting possibility that what they are doing can make a profound difference in the lives of their families, friends, colleagues, clients, patients, congregations, and communities.

Nils Hansen, in his Personal-Best Leadership Experience on an eCommerce project within a multinational retail organization, realized that "finding a common purpose within the team dynamic could instill a strong sense of meaning and satisfaction for everyone involved." His first step was "genuinely getting to know my team members as individuals," he told us. "What are their aspirations? What do they care about in life? Do they see themselves somewhere specific in the next 12 months? At the pinnacle of their careers?" Nils got to know everyone on his team and learned that each was a passionate video game user outside of work. The products they were in the business of selling were products for which they had a personal affinity. "This personal appreciation for our product," he said, "was incredibly powerful and something that was invaluable in tying us all to the shared vision."

Studies involving respondents from 40 different countries (and 16 different languages) found that connecting employees with purpose increased their levels of engagement and productivity.[6] Similarly, the LPI data reveals that individuals who are seen as very frequently or nearly always showing people how enlisting in a common vision can help them achieve their long-term interests are evaluated 15 times more favorably by their peers than those individuals who engage in this same leadership behavior rarely, if at all. Researchers have shown that stressing the "why" to people, as in "Why are we doing this and why does it matter?" activates the brain's reward system and increases how favorably people feel about what they are doing, as well as increasing their efforts.[7]

Take Pride in Being Unique   Visions should also communicate what sets your team, workplace, or community apart from others. There's no advantage in being on a team or working for an institution that does precisely the same thing as the one across town. If you want people to sign up with you, they first have to understand how what you are proposing is distinctive and stands out from the crowd. Uniqueness fosters pride. It boosts the self-respect and self-esteem of everyone associated with the endeavor. The prouder people are of the place they work or the community where they live, the more engaged they're likely to be.

Holly Waxman worked in a prestigious university research laboratory with world-renowned scientists. She and her colleagues were responsible for making sure that all the equipment was operating properly, and even though some seemed not to regard that work as prestigious as that of the scientists, she told us how she made sure to keep the spirits of her colleagues up by letting them know that what they were doing was still quite special and made a unique contribution: "After all, the work that is being done can impact the health of many people, improving their quality of life. Keeping the equipment up and running is crucial because this actually makes the research possible."

Her motivating perspective was similar to Matt Kendrick's, a facilities engineer in a regional hospital, who told his colleagues: "By keeping the HVAC (heating, ventilation, air conditioning) working, we make it possible for people to recover more quickly from their illnesses and return back to their homes." Take the opportunity, whenever possible, to share your sense of pride in the contribution your work makes to the larger organizational mission. Just talking about what makes you proud sparks those same feelings in others. Hearing from peers about the pride they have in their work is contagious. They come to share the delight you express.

You excite people about enlisting in a shared vision by making sure that all involved feel that what they do is unique and believe that they play a crucial role, regardless of job titles or specific task responsibilities. Azmeena Zaveri learned just how important it is for people to take pride in being unique when she led a team of volunteers in handling the sales and finances of a community bookstore in Karachi, Pakistan. The bookstore was an iconic, celebrated, and cherished institution where people had loved to gather to socialize and learn. When Azmeena agreed to take on the financial management role, however, the bookstore was in survival mode. It was no longer providing a high standard of service, there was a lack of conscientiousness in the management of the finances, and there was little motivation to go the extra mile. The reason for the decline "was not because the team was incompetent or incapable of managing the tasks," she told us. "A principal cause was the lack of vision and direction for the team. My goal was to inspire the team to bring the bookstore back to being the place where people loved to go, not just because of the great collection of books, but also for the inviting vibe and sense of community."

Azmeena coached the volunteers on ways to improve the bookkeeping process, talked about how to better utilize the store's scarce resources, and told them how much the patrons relied on the bookstore as an important part of their lives. Throughout the process, she said she "emphasized how the institution was relying on them to survive and retain its significance to the community, and how they were in an honorable position to not just serve a bookstore, but be a community icon with an esteemed legacy."

Focusing on uniqueness makes it possible for smaller units within large organizations, or individual neighborhoods within big cities, to have their visions and still serve a larger, collective vision. Although every unit within a corporation, public agency, religious institution, school, or volunteer association must align with the overall organizational vision, each can express its unique purpose within the larger whole and highlight its most distinguishing qualities. Each can be proud of its ideal image of its future as it works toward the collective future of the larger organization.

Create Images of the Future   Visions are images in the mind; they are impressions and representations. A beacon of light cutting through the fog is an image you can picture in your mind. You make these images real to others by expressing them in concrete and vivid terms. As shown in Figure 3, the more frequently that individuals are seen by their colleagues as "describing a compelling image of what our future could look like," the more their peers strongly agree that they really care about the long-term success of the organization.

In our workshops and classes, we often use an exercise to illustrate the power of painting word pictures. It goes like this: We ask people to think about the city of Paris, France, and to shout out the first thing that comes to mind. The replies—the Eiffel Tower, the Arc de Triomphe, the Seine, Notre Dame, good food, wine, romance—are all images of real places, experiences, and emotions. No one calls out the kilometers, population, or gross domestic product of Paris. The same would be true for your team or organization. The reason for this is that human memory is stored in images and sensory impressions, not in numbers. People recall images of reality, not abstractions from reality.

When you speak about the future, long before the journey begins you need to get a mental picture of what things will be like when you

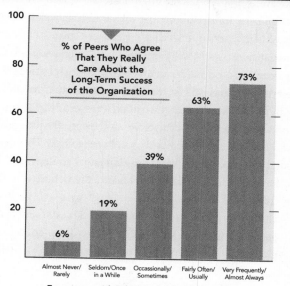

Figure 3 Showing Others That Their Long-Term Interests Can Be Realized by Enlisting in a Common Vision Results in Peers Caring More About the Organization's Success

% of Peers Who Agree That They Really Care About the Long-Term Success of the Organization

Frequency with Which Individual Shows Others How Their Long-Term Interests Can Be Realized by Enlisting in a Common Vision

arrive at your destination. Images are your windows on the world of tomorrow. When talking about going places people have never been, you start by imagining what this would look like. You literally paint a picture of the future and make manifest the purpose so that others can see it, hear it, taste it, touch it, feel it.

Janet Lopez told us she was with the behavioral health unit of a national HMO when she used captivating images to spark people's interest in implementing online platforms for health education, "and most importantly, painting a vivid picture with words of what our future would look like by reaching those patients who faced challenges and barriers to treatment." She explained, "I was specific in how I could see each of their strengths contributing to this vision, and how I saw them playing a role in the 'big picture' of the work that we wanted to accomplish." Leaders like Janet understand that painting a picture of the future requires making full use of the power of language in communicating a shared identity and giving life to visions. They use metaphors and other figures of speech to provide vividness and tangibility to abstract ideas. They use descriptive language, give examples, tell stories, and relate anecdotes in expressing their hopes for the future. In making the intangible vision tangible, they ignite constituents' passion, developing a shared sense of destiny.

Your challenge is to literally see what is often someone else's vision— like your manager's, the department's, or the organization's—and then finding ways to express this so that those around you can also envision. While Sean Collins serves as his small college's director of environment, health, and safety, no one reports to him and his leadership involves helping others, like the faculty, to embrace a culture of safety. He often achieves this through imagery, asking laboratory directors to imagine what might happen if a host of safety protocols were not followed, or how their research would be affected if the lab were shut down by an inspection agency. Making sure that his colleagues could see what he could see was central to moving from lip service about ensuring that students do not get hurt to everyone taking actions to hold themselves accountable to safety standards.

There are no freeways to the future, and often all you can do as a leader is to have a "theme" and a set of values and principles that enable you to have some sense of what might be possible, and at best, this is often just an image. The key is getting others to imagine in their minds' eye the image of what could be, how it could be, and why it must be. Janet Lopez realized that her colleagues were buying into the vision she had articulated when they started to share ideas about what might be possible, how they might contribute, and the pilot projects they could launch. She described "group members brainstorming about ways we could address confidentiality issues, appeal to management for funding, and even spark outside investors." Janet noticed how powerful creating images of the future can be: "There was excitement in the air, with smiles and forward-leaning body language when everyone was engaged in imagining our future."

Practice Positive Communication and Be Expressive

Our research shows that people want to follow those who are enthusiastic, exude energy, and have a positive attitude. Upbeat people attract others and convey the feeling that the journey will be invigorating and the leader is in it for the long haul. People follow those with a can-do attitude and not those cynics who give ten reasons why something is impossible or who don't make others feel good about themselves or what they're doing.

Researchers have documented that people actually remember downbeat comments far more often, in greater detail and with more intensity, than they do encouraging words.[8] When negative remarks become a preoccupation, people's brains lose mental efficiency. This is all the more reason that you need to look on the bright side. A positive approach to life broadens people's ideas about future possibilities, and these exciting options build on each other.[9] In an affirming environment, people become more innovative and see more options. Positivity increases your ability to cope with adversity and be more resilient during times of high stress.

Randi DuBois, one of the founders of an experiential outdoor training organization, gets people to literally stretch what they think they are capable of doing by having them engage in challenging physical tasks. Typically, her clients are nervous, even a bit scared at first. But people of all ages, all sizes, and all physical abilities have successfully completed their outdoor challenge courses. How does Randi succeed in leading these people? Her secret is very simple: She's always positive that people can do the course, and she never says "never." We've watched her in programs as she conveys very clearly, and often, that people have the power within themselves to accomplish whatever they desire; to do things they never imagined themselves doing. Being positive opens people up to seeing more options, to being more willing to experiment, and to be focused on learning.

In explaining why they are magnetically attracted to particular leaders, people often describe them as charismatic. But *charisma* has become such an overused and misused term that it's almost useless as a descriptor of leaders. For instance, leadership scholars note that "in the popular media, charisma has come to mean anything ranging from chutzpah to Pied Piperism, from celebrity to Superman status. It has become an overworked cliché for a strong, attractive, and inspiring personality."[10]

To better understand what this elusive quality is, social scientists have observed the behavior of individuals, like Randi, who are deemed to be charismatic. What they've found is that people who are perceived to be charismatic are just more animated than others. They smile more, speak faster, pronounce words more clearly, and move their heads and bodies more often. They are also more likely to reach out and touch or make some physical contact with others during greetings.[11] The most successful talks on TED.com are made by presenters who use almost twice as many hand gestures as their less-viewed peers.[12] Studies using animated stick figures as the speakers showed that those judged to be most energetic and enthusiastic employed many more hand movements overall, and their physical movements were predictive of those who received the most applause from their audience.[13]

Accordingly, *being charismatic* can better be understood as the willingness to be expressive. And the more expressive you are, the more likely those around you are likely to be infected by your enthusiasm, or as one clinical nurse described in her Personal-Best Leadership Experience: "I was contagiously enthusiastic, and so positive about the possibilities of this new surgical procedure, that others got on board even before they knew all the details."

We've found that people often underestimate their abilities to be expressive, as easily evidenced by their performance when talking about their Personal-Best Leadership Experiences or about their ideal futures, or even their upcoming holidays and vacations. When relating hopes, dreams, and successes, people are almost always emotionally expressive. They lean forward in their chairs, they move their arms about, eyes light up, voices sing with excitement, and they smile.

Being energetic and expressive are key descriptors of what it means to be charismatic. The old saying that enthusiasm is infectious is certainly true for leaders. By adding emotion to your words and behavior, you can increase the likelihood that people will remember what you say and act upon it. You need to share the enthusiasm you have with others, rather than locking it away and assuming that expressiveness is somehow "unprofessional."

None of these suggestions about being positive and more expressive will be of any value whatsoever if you don't believe in what you're saying. If the vision is someone else's and you don't own it, you'll have a tough time enlisting others in it. If you have trouble imagining yourself living the future described in the vision, you certainly will not be able to convince others that they ought to enlist in making it a reality. If you're not excited about the possibilities, you can't expect others to be. The prerequisite to enlisting others in a shared vision is genuineness.

Take Action to Inspire a Shared Vision

Visions give focus to human energy, they set the agenda giving direction and purpose. They enable each person connected with the work to see more clearly what's ahead of them and what the future will look like when everyone has added their piece. Shared visions keep everyone focused, and with this in mind, people can contribute to the whole, efficiently and with confidence.

However, visions seen only by the leader are insufficient to generate organized movement. You must also get others to see a way forward, one that is filled with exciting possibilities that lie ahead. You must breathe life into visions, not only by your own enthusiasm and expressiveness but by listening to and communicating the hopes and dreams of others so that they clearly understand how their values and interests will be served. Speaking with authenticity about your own convictions and the uniqueness of your organization makes others proud to be part of something special. Being upbeat and expressive attracts followers through your energy, optimism, and sincerity.

In the next chapter we explain how you create a climate in which you can develop the innovative ideas and processes that will be needed to realize a shared vision of the future. We'll explore how you Challenge the Process by searching for opportunities and experimenting and taking risks.

Here are two recommended actions that you should take to continuously strengthen your competence in the leadership practice of Inspire a Shared Vision:

Envision the Future. You can broaden your understanding of future trends by making sure you're seeking out diverse points of view. Take the time to initiate discussions with co-workers about the future and where your organization may fit into it; ask how they think your organization might stay competitive and which ideas might be implemented now. Reach out and talk to others outside your group and company, and, if possible, include conversing with customers and clients about what they need and want. Listen for clues in every conversation you have. Any good dream of the future will be rooted in conversations that are likely happening already every day—you just need to figure out how to tune into them! Talking and listening go hand-in-hand, and ultimately, engaging others in dialogues will enrich your understanding of what the future might hold and how best to tackle it.

Enlist Others. In order to get colleagues, teammates, or friends on board with new ideas or initiatives when the opportunity arises you need to know something about their interests and aspirations. Initiate conversations with them about their dreams and hopes, and about which of the organization's ideals are most important to them. Ask them why they joined the group or team in the first place, why they felt it was a place they could thrive. What gets them up in the morning, and ignites their passion? Determine the ways in which their visions of the future intersect with your own. Emphasize those areas of overlap when you describe what you hope to achieve, helping them to appreciate how there are shared aspirations. Aim to get them just as revved up as you are about the worth of the work that you are all doing.

Challenge
the Process

CHAPTER 4

Challenge
the Process

YOU NEVER KNOW where or when the opportunity for leadership will arise. Certainly, this was the case for Jenna Wingate, who back in 2014 was a part-time zookeeper at the Cincinnati Zoo and Botanical Garden. When one of her colleagues decided to create a local chapter of the American Association of Zoo Keepers (AAZK), Jenna was right beside her. They obviously needed to recruit members from their fellow animal care workers, but they were also required to participate in the national organization's annual fundraising event, Bowling for Rhinos. It was here that Jenna stepped up and provided leadership in helping her newly formed chapter make a measurable and lasting impact.

Though neither a formal event planner nor experienced fundraiser, Jenna jumped into the bowling event with great excitement. With the number of nonprofit organizations seeking sponsorships and funding, and almost all utilizing professional fundraisers, she knew her team's approach had to be distinctively different. "The whole thing was mostly a 'figure it out as you go' endeavor," Jenna explained.

> My colleagues suggested several ideas for raising money and how to attract sponsors and donors. But we had no way of knowing in advance if any of them would work. For example,

we decided to create different sponsorship levels—ranging from a company name and logo on a T-shirt, to personalized tours with animals at the Cincinnati Zoo. We had no idea if we were appropriately matching the donation amount with the benefit, we just agreed to experiment, learn, and move forward.

We knew that to promote the event we had to do something other than simply sending generic email announcements and adding postings on social media. So I organized some happy hours where a bunch of us would socialize and talk about how important Bowling for Rhinos was, and then we would head out in small groups, literally cold-calling small businesses, restaurants, and "Mom and Pops." It was always scary and awkward asking for money, but doing it in these small groups really helped us get after it.

Jenna told us that she and her colleagues tried a lot of things. Some ideas worked out and some didn't, but added that "We just learned from the mistakes and missteps and then tried something else. Although it is funny now, we learned from our first bake sale not to sell desserts outside in the summer heat of July. Icing melts."

There were several risks inherent in this first-time fundraising event, not the least of which was whether they could actually get people to donate, especially because they weren't allowed to solicit from any of the current Cincinnati Zoo's donors. So Jenna looked outside the organization's philanthropic foundations and community benefactors. For example, she reached out to various contractors working at the zoo, who reached out to their subcontractors, who reached out to their friends. Another risk was how high to set their fundraising goal. The chapter president, in fact, thought they were being too ambitious! And for Jenna herself, if this event was not successful, she worried about how it might impact the way she would be viewed in her day job with the Zoo. Yet for Jenna, the potential payoff was always worth the risks; their efforts were for such a good cause.

Across the entire AAZK network, it commonly took about six years for long-running chapters to hit $2,000 in funding for Bowling for Rhinos. In their first year, the Cincinnati chapter raised $9,000, and five years later, through silent auctions, merchandise sales, and raffles, increased this amount to $35,000. This was the largest contribution from any chapter that year, including those from much larger zoos such as St. Louis, San Diego, and the Bronx. Much of this success occurred because of the genuinely new ways of thinking that Jenna brought to what Bowling for Rhinos could be.[1]

As Jenna's story demonstrates, you don't have to be at the top of the organization to suggest and implement new ideas that result in accomplishing something no other organization like yours has achieved. What you do have to do is to take the initiative and then persevere. Leadership is not about maintaining the status quo or doing what everyone else is doing. Encouraging yourself and others to venture outside of job descriptions and role stereotypes and exploring options beyond current limits, standards, and norms are key to making extraordinary things happen. The challenges and opportunities of today and tomorrow demand a willingness to take risks and experiment with innovative ideas. Leaders foster risk taking rather than playing it safe and encourage others to step out into the unknown. They set goals that are higher than current levels, but not so steep that people feel only frustration and disappointment. They do not challenge just for the sake of change but challenge with the purposeful aspiration to improve and, like Jenna, to make things better for a just cause.

When people describe their Personal-Best Leadership Experiences they invariably talk about times of significant change, even though that's not what we asked them about. It turns out that no one ever did their personal-best by keeping things the same. The fact is that when times are stable and secure, people are not severely tested. You may perform well, be promoted, even achieve some fame and fortune. But certainty and routine breed complacency. In times of calm, you do not feel any compulsions to look deep inside and discover untapped talents and passions buried there. In contrast, personal and organizational hardships have a way of making you come face-to-face with who you really are and what you are capable of becoming. Leadership is inherently associated with change and challenge. It involves doing things differently, a loftier goal than simply settling for the way things are. Without challenge you are unlikely to change, and without change, you cannot lead yourself or your colleagues to greatness.

The most effective leaders are those who most frequently engage in the Challenge the Process leadership practice. Individuals asked their colleagues to complete the LPI–Observer, indicating how often they observed that person engaging in the six leadership behaviors associated with Challenge the Process. Peers were also asked for an assessment of how effective they found this individual to be as a leader. The statistical analysis showed that effectiveness evaluations increased systematically as peers indicated this individual engaging more and more frequently in these leadership behaviors.

Seize the Initiative to Improve

The vast majority of organizations, institutions, and even communities and families are not typically bastions of change; often quite the contrary. People generally cling to what's familiar, they can be slow to adopt new systems and processes, and traditions are often sacred. Doing better than you are doing right now requires you to Challenge the Process. This is not about challenge just for the sake of change, but change for the sake of something better. Leaders are motivated by the desire to make extraordinary, not ordinary, things happen. Making the current situation better demands change. It would be foolish to expect things to be better just by doing what has always been done over and over again.

The work of leaders is associated with adversity, uncertainty, hardship, disruption, transformation, transition, recovery, and new beginnings. Sometimes the changes are small, sometimes they are large, but they are all about awakening new possibilities. Leaders don't always have to change history, but they do have to make a change in the "business as usual" mindset.

The lasting changes that Marion Krause made at a small consulting company were clearly outside of her job description. A devoted environmentalist, Marion believed strongly in recycling and other citizen actions that make the world a cleaner, more beautiful place for her son, Benjamin, and for everyone else. She wasn't the founder, an officer, or a manager of the firm, but when she arrived at this company as the office administrator she noticed that there was no recycling of compost, paper, bottles, cans, or plastic products. Had there been a poll, everyone would have agreed that they should recycle; the trouble was, no one had taken the initiative to do anything about it. Marion did. She gathered all the necessary bins and boxes, demonstrated what and how to recycle, and persisted in carrying the banner for this change until it became a daily habit. Not only is leadership everyone's business, but it is also true, as Marion's experience demonstrates, that leadership is about taking the initiative to make a difference.

The LPI data backs up this observation. Those individuals who were seen by their peers as "taking initiative in anticipating and responding to change" were also viewed as bringing out the best of people's talents and abilities (Figure 4).

In our research, we also asked people about "What five or six words would you use to best describe the character—the feel, the spirit, the nature, the quality—of your Personal-Best Leadership Experience?" The words most frequently used have been *challenging, rewarding,* and *exciting.* Words signifying conviction (*dedication, intensity, commitment, determination,* and *persistence*) and passion (*inspiring, uplifting, motivating,* and *energizing*) are also mentioned regularly. *Unique, important, proud,* and *empowering* got their fair share as well. Fully 95 percent of the cases were described in these terms. No one ever used the word *boring.* Neither did anyone use *dull, unsatisfying, ordinary, disinterested, indifferent, apathetic,* or *routine.* Humdrum situations simply aren't associated with personal-best performances.

These responses suggest a highly spirited outlook associated with leadership. All of the descriptions are vibrant and full of life. The personal bests were times when people felt fully alive. You need to seize the initiative with enthusiasm and determination, focus on uplifting human

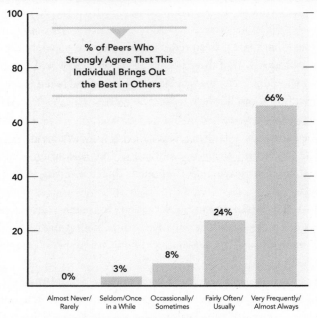

Figure 4 Individuals Who Take Initiative in Anticipating and Responding to Change Are Seen by Their Peers as Bringing Out the Best in Others

Frequency with Which Individual Takes Initiative
in Anticipating and Responding to Change

endeavors, and have an internal desire to make something happen. The leaders in our study embraced the challenge presented by the disruptions in their industries, new demands of the marketplace, and pressing needs in their communities.

Of course, change is never easy. Sometimes leadership bests were described as stressful, frustrating, frightening, or anxiety-producing. But instead of being debilitated by the pressure of a difficult challenge, people were stimulated and energized by it. Stress always accompanies the pursuit of excellence, but when you are doing your best it never overtakes you. Disruptive change demands significant commitment and sacrifice, but the positive feelings associated with forward progress generates momentum that enables people to ride out the storm.

Make Something Happen   When asked about who initiated the projects that they selected as their Personal-Best Leadership Experiences, it was initially surprising that most people did not name themselves. More than half the cases were initiated by someone else. In the workplace, it was usually the person's immediate supervisor. It was also often the situation—such as a crisis, equipment or system failure, performance/revenue gap, technology disruption, customer turnover, sickness, or something else outside of the leader's personal control.

But if leadership is about seizing the initiative, then how can people be called leaders when they are assigned the jobs and tasks they undertake or if they are simply responding to a situation? The fact is that much of what people do in work organizations is assigned; few get to start anything from scratch, select all of their colleagues, or make strategic decisions about the organization's products and the community's services. The reality is that most challenges choose you and not the other way around. The finding that over half the cases were not self-initiated is actually quite positive and reassuring. It liberates those who are weighted down by thinking that they have to start all the changes themselves. It underscores the point that people can be exemplary leaders, even if they are not the individuals who start a business or develop a revolutionary invention or spearhead a change movement. Everyone has the chance to lead if they choose to take what they've been given and make something extraordinary happen. Everyone can be responsible for innovation and improvement. If the only times people reported doing their best were when they got to be the founder, supervisor, director, or some "head honcho," the majority of leadership experiences would evaporate—as would the majority of change in society.

Nothing could stifle innovation more than accepting the axiom that "If it ain't broke, don't fix it." Something always needs fixing in every organization, every community, every school, and every home. Go find what needs fixing in yours. Taking on a new job or new assignment is an ideal opportunity to ask probing questions and challenging the way things are done. Those are the times when you are expected to ask, "Why do we do this?" But don't just ask this when you're new to the job; make this a routine question. Treat today as if it were your first day. Ask yourself, "If I were just starting this job or task, what would I do differently?" Then do those things immediately.

Don't stop with what you can find on your own. Ask your colleagues about what really bugs them about what's going on. Ask them what gets in the way of doing the best job possible. Take time to periodically wander around the plant, the store, the branch, the shop, the hallways, the office, or the neighborhood and look for things that don't seem right. Ask questions. Probe. These are ways that you will continuously uncover needed improvements, or at least gather clues about what might need some attention.

The research evidence indicates that people who rate high in proactivity are assessed by their immediate managers as more effective leaders.[2] Students who rate high on being proactive are also considered by their peers to be better leaders; in addition, they are more engaged in extracurricular and civic activities targeted toward bringing about positive change.[3] Similar results about the connection between proactivity and performance have been found among entrepreneurs, administrative staff, and college students searching for jobs. Proactivity consistently produces better results than reactivity or inactivity.[4]

You make something happen when you notice what isn't working, create a possible solution for the problem, gain buy-in from constituents, and implement the desired outcome. When thinking back on his early career experiences as a financial analyst, Varun Mundra realized an added benefit: "When I did question the status quo, when I did come up with innovative ideas, when I followed through with the changes I suggested, got feedback, understood my mistakes, learned from them, and was open to improvements, I won the respect of the people around me." To repeat: When Varun questioned the status quo, he won the respect of his peers. What's holding you back? As they say in basketball, none of the shots you *don't* take ever go in the hoop. You've got to make something happen—to shoot the ball—in order to score some points. That's the key insight Varun had when he took the initiative, "It did not matter as much whether the changes were as effective as hoped for," he told us, "but the fact that someone was ready to stand up and challenge what everyone else used as the norm was generally enough to get something started."

Seizing initiative has less to do with position than it does with attitude and action. Innovation and excellence are the results of people at all levels making things happen. When it comes to change and continuous improvement, people need to believe that they can take the initiative to do something different. Opportunities to challenge the status quo and introduce change create the opportunities for doing your best. Challenge is the motivating environment for excellence. It's not so important whether you find the challenges or they find you. What is important are the choices you make. The question to ask yourself is: When opportunity knocks, am I prepared to answer the door?

Make Challenge Meaningful   What gets *you* going in the morning, eager to embrace whatever might be in store for the day? What motivates *you* to do your best, day in and day out? Why do people push their limits to get extraordinary things done? And for that matter, why do people do many things for little or no tangible rewards? Why do they volunteer to put out fires, raise money for worthy causes, or help children in need? Why do people join Sister Mary Prema Pierick, M.C., in caring for the poorest of the poor? Why do they risk their careers to start a new business or risk their security to change the social condition? Why do they sign up for AmeriCorps, the Peace Corps, or Médecins Sans Frontières (Doctors Without Borders)? Extrinsic rewards—the traditional cliché of "what gets rewarded gets done"—certainly can't explain these actions. You cannot pay people to care about their products and services, customers, clients or patients, productivity, profitability or safety, colleagues, or even their friends and family.

A sense of meaning and purpose is what gets people through the tough times, the times when they don't think they can even get up in the morning or take another step, give another lecture, analyze another set of data, debug another line of code, generate another sales lead, write another strategic report, load another package, refurbish another room, attend another rally, game, or concert, organize another reception or vendor exhibit, hold another recruitment or orientation session, and on and on. The motivation to deal with the challenges and uncertainties of life and work comes from the inside and not from something that others hold out as some kind of carrot.

From the analysis of Personal-Best Leadership Experiences, the motivation was not about challenge simply for the sake of challenge, or just rocking the boat, or taking on the role of devil's advocate or nay-sayer. Babies may be the only people who really like and appreciate "being changed." You need to have a reason for changing that addresses the traditional thinking of "if it ain't broke, why fix it." Meaning often comes from looking beyond daily problems and happens when there is a chance to do something that is internally motivating.

It's evident from our research, and from studies by many others, that if people are going to do their best, the task or project in which they are involved must be intrinsically engaging.[5] When it comes to excellence, it's definitely *not* "what gets rewarded gets done"; it's "what *is* rewarding gets done." Researchers have conducted extensive studies to explore the nature of activities that contain rewards within themselves.[6] They explain that people enjoyed their chosen activity because of the pleasure they derived both from the experience and from using their skills. Extrinsic rewards, like power, prestige, and glamour, were ranked least important. Their conclusion was that whatever the specific structure of an intrinsically rewarding task, "it seems that its most basic requirement is to provide a clear set of challenges."[7] People who justify their employment on solely economic grounds will seldom contribute more than the minimum. A key factor in making challenge meaningful, and tapping into intrinsic motivation, is to get yourself and others to look around in new ways.

Look Outward for Fresh Ideas Accepting new challenges means living with high degrees of ambiguity. Change and the accompanying uncertainty upset stability and throw off customary equilibrium. Yet it's these fluctuations, disturbances, and imbalances that are the primary sources of creativity.[8] Routines are often the enemies of change. So are established procedures and demands—all those memoranda, telephone calls, reports, meetings, plans, emails, and the like. You can get so busy in the day-to-day details of your work that you become ensnared in an activity trap, where you are very busy but not making much progress.

So where do you find pioneering ideas? The good news is that you don't have to come up with them on your own. Look around and listen, because innovations can come from just about anywhere. Sometimes they come from your customers, from suppliers, from the R&D labs, from the people doing the work, from disruptive technologies, from seminars, from your competitors, and so on. The point is that there is no shortage of possible ideas. You must find ways that keep you in touch with trends in your discipline, profession, and industry marketplaces, with the viewpoints and perspectives of people from a variety of backgrounds and functions, and with ongoing social, political, technological, economic, and artistic changes. Be aware of and open to what's going on around you. Be sensitive to even the fuzziest sign or weakest signal that there's something possibly new on the horizon.

Researchers shadowing senior executives discovered that the most successful ones were not waiting for information to come to them.[9] Instead, they were out and about gathering knowledge so that they could understand what to do next, and you can begin doing the same. Omer Ali Rao says the questions that have bothered him throughout his professional career are "Why do we do things the way we do? and Why don't we ask questions if we are not clear?" He took these questions to heart in his Personal-Best Leadership Experience, having been hired to advise directly the CEO of an investment company in Saudi Arabia on their portfolio. He began by "exhaustively" studying the current protocols, observing the work culture and diversity of the team, examining the company's internal political environment, and so on. He "engaged in open discussions with colleagues, and then with directors," testing ideas in an iterative process, before presenting any recommendations to the CEO. Now working with a North American organization providing roadside emergency services, Omer continued this practice of looking outward for fresh ideas. For example, to better understand how technology could remove inefficiencies, he spent a few weeks riding along on their tow trucks, talking with the drivers about their experiences, and observing first-hand interactions with stranded motorists.

Unless people actively seek diverse points of view and engage with others outside their usual channels of communication, over time they will interact less and less frequently with outsiders and become cut off from new ideas and ways of thinking. Classic studies have revealed a strong relationship between the effectiveness of a team and its communications with group members, others in the organization, and professionals outside the company.[10] Each team's technical performance was measured by department managers and laboratory directors. The higher-performing teams had significantly more communication with people outside their workplaces, whether with organizational units such as marketing and manufacturing or with outside professional associations. The poor-performing teams reported lower levels of communications in all three areas, essentially cutting themselves off from sources that could provide the most critical kinds of feedback, suggestions, and technological advances. They isolated themselves from information available within other organizational divisions.

One of the reasons that people are often afraid to ask around for advice and input from others is because they perceive that doing so means, or at least implies, that they're incompetent or don't know something that they should already know. However, studies have shown that this fear is misplaced. Research documents that people perceive those who seek advice as more competent than those who do not seek help, and this belief is even stronger when the task is difficult than when it is easy.[11]

If you are going to detect opportunities for change—before those opportunities wither, become demands, or create huge problems—you must use your *outsight*. Outsight is the sibling of insight, and it means being able to perceive external realities. Without outsight, innovation cannot happen. And insight without outsight is like seeing clearly with blinders on; you just won't get a complete picture. Studies into how the brain processes information suggest that in order to see things differently and more creatively, you have to bombard your brain with things it has never encountered. Novelty is vital, explain neuroscientists, because the brain, evolved for efficiency, routinely takes perceptual shortcuts to save energy. Only by forcing yourself to break free of preexisting views can you get your brain to re-categorize information. Moving beyond habitual thinking patterns is the starting point to imagining truly novel alternatives.[12]

To get a good sense of the external realities, you have to get up from your desk, go out of your office, and spend time outside of your usual discipline or functional field. For example, attend a conference in an entirely different arena from your own, takes a class in a different field, tour facilities in industries with which you are unfamiliar; see the world through a different lens. Put yourself into new situations that force you to examine and confront your existing paradigms. Consider "associating," a discovery skill linked with innovators, which involves making connections across "seemingly unrelated questions, problems, or ideas."[13] Consider how you might stir imagination by starting a discussion with your colleagues about such questions as: How would Disney handle our customer relationships? How would Southwest Airlines develop our recruitment and on-boarding programs? How would Amazon design our inventory system?

Experiment and Take Risks

When we talk about Challenge the Process, you might be getting the impression that you have to start "big." That's not necessarily true. Change conceived of too broadly can be so overwhelming that you can't even figure out where or how to start. Just thinking about gigantic problems can defeat your capacity to even imagine what might be done, let alone strengthen the determination required to solve them. Framing the challenge, problem, or opportunity as too immense can actually have the effect of dampening motivation to do anything. Boldness is not necessarily about go-for-broke, giant-leap projects. More often than not it is about starting small and gaining momentum.

Break big problems and projects into small, doable steps, and it becomes easier to get the people involved to say "yes" numerous times. Small, visible steps are much more likely to lead to early victories than big-bang efforts. They also gain early supporters. Within the scientific and academic communities there has always been an understanding that major breakthroughs are likely to be the result of the work of scores of researchers, as countless contributions finally begin to add up to a solution. Taking the sum total of all the "little" improvements in technology, regardless of the industry, has been shown to contribute more to a substantial increase in organizational productivity than all the great inventors and their inventions.[14] Progress is more likely to be the result of a focus on incremental improvements in tools and processes than of tectonic shifts of minds. This is also the case for individual change as researchers have shown that the place to start in creating long-term changes in your behavior is by taking small actions, often taking less than 30 seconds.[15] Often a small and unobtrusive nudge in the right direction can lead to people eating better, saving more for retirement, and conserving energy.[16] Therefore, to get people to *want* to change the way they're currently headed, you need to nurture an experimental attitude and begin with a one-step-at-a-time approach. As an old African proverb advises: "Never test the depth of the water with both feet."

Of course, when you experiment, not everything works out as intended, so you have to make taking risks safe. Mistakes and false starts are both a natural and necessary part of the process of innovation and leadership. What's critical is capturing the learning generated from these experiences.

Make It Safe to Take Risks   It seems obviously paradoxical, but the truth is that unless people feel sufficiently safe they will be unwilling, even unable, to experiment and take risks. The concept of "psychological safety" refers to the experience of feeling able to speak up with relevant ideas, questions, or concerns, and is not a personality factor but rather a workplace characteristic. An environment in which there is mutual trust and respect nurtures candor and a sense of obligation to communicate when there are disagreements, as well as opportunities.[17] People believe that if they make a mistake, or ask for help, their colleagues will not think less of them, pick them apart, ridicule or punish them. Fear inhibits people from venturing outside of their comfort zones and impedes information-sharing, asking for help, or experimenting. They remain silent even when they believe they have something to say that has the potential of adding value. People do not do their best when they are afraid, as research in neuroscience shows that fear consumes physiologic resources, impairing analytic thinking, creative insight, and problem solving.[18] This situation has been likened to the difference between playing not to lose (avoiding losses) and playing to win (seeking gains).[19] Playing not to lose is a mindset that focuses, consciously but often not, on protecting against the downside (embarrassment, ridicule, security); playing to win is focused on the upside, seeking opportunity, and necessarily means taking risks.

There is plenty of empirical evidence that psychological safety matters both personally and organizationally, affecting everything from employee error reporting to return on investment.[20] A multiple-year study of over 180 teams at Google found that no mix of personality types, skills, backgrounds, or matches with the work expected helped explain which teams performed well and which did not. Psychological safety was the critical factor explaining why some teams outperformed others.[21] In a study of more than 20,000 people around the world, the O.C. Tanner Institute reported that when employees feel safe there is a 347 percent increase in the probability of highly-engaged employees, 154 percent increase in great work, and a 33 percent decrease in moderate-to-severe burnout.[22]

If, you're not the person at the top of your organization, so what can you do to create psychological safety for yourself and your colleagues? One strategy is to ask questions that invite participation and take the initiative to address what might be people's reluctant silence and possible defensiveness. For example, instead of asking, "What mistakes did people notice when we did xyz?" consider reframing the question along these lines: "Did we do everything as well as we could have when we did xyz?" See what you can do to speak up yourself and make others comfortable doing so. Foster a "humble mindset," which focuses on what can be learned rather than simply what didn't work and who might be to blame.[23] This means being willing to acknowledge your own fallibility and shortcomings. Assuming a modest level of good will in your organization, according to researchers, pays off: "Most of the time your colleagues will respond well to genuine expressions of vulnerability and interest."[24]

Karina Chamorro, as a law school registration coordinator, served on a cross-functional project team tasked with building a new student system, and remembers how self-conscious she was at the start of this Personal-Best Leadership Experience. Since she was much younger and less experienced than the rest of the team, she felt compelled to reach out to her colleagues and learn from them. She met one-on-one with project teammates: "I intended to absorb their experience and knowledge like a sponge, and I was unafraid to position myself as a learner. I found that people appreciated being recognized as experts with their unique perspectives. The unexpected outcome was that these interactions also built personal connections and a foundation of trust." Establishing these direct relationships and open communication channels early in the project, she said, "helped me gain a sense of psychological safety in larger group meetings where age, gender, and hierarchical dynamics felt dominant at first."

It's true, as Karina experienced, that by asking questions you create a space for other people to contribute their thinking. This conveys your interest in their perspectives and respect for their opinions. Show a genuine interest in what others are saying by asking them to tell you more about their thinking and experiences: "Can you say more about that?" or "Can you give an example?" Test for consensus rather than assuming that silence means agreement. Ask questions like, "Who has a different perspective?" or "What might we not be taking into account?" Show that you are interested in what others have to contribute by letting them know that you are available to help.

Finally, show appreciation rather than judgment for people taking risks; for example, "Thank you for speaking up about this matter or option." It takes courage to speak up and you need to acknowledge that. When people believe that their performance is an indicator of a fixed degree of ability or intelligence, they are less likely to take any risks than when they come to believe that performance reflects a cumulative ability to learn and grow from experience. In the latter case they are eager to try new things and willing to persevere despite adversity and setbacks.

Make Small Wins Work The incremental change process has been called "small wins," and each success builds people's commitment to a course of action.[25] Small wins form a consistent pattern of accomplishment that attracts people who want to be allied with a successful venture, building their confidence and reinforcing their natural desire to feel successful. Since additional resources tend to flow to winners, a small win means that slightly larger steps or wins can be attempted next. A series of small wins contributes to constructing a stable foundation on which bigger risks can be taken. Each win offers information that facilitates learning and adaptation.

Small wins also deter opposition for the simple reason that it is hard to argue against success. Thus, small wins decrease resistance to subsequent proposals. With the achievement of a small win, natural forces are set in motion that propel actions toward another small win. This simple strategy of winning step-by-step succeeds more often than massive overhauls and gigantic projects. It's not just that it's easier, it is also because personal and group commitment is built in the process. Planting one tree won't stop global warming, but planting one million trees one at a time can make a significant difference. Planting that first tree starts things. The visible success shows others that they too can plant a tree and make a difference.

Getting the sense that they are daily making progress in meaningful work triggers people's intrinsic motivation. As Harvard researchers have reported, "When we think of progress, we often imagine how good it feels to achieve a long-term goal or experience a major breakthrough. These big wins are great—but they are relatively rare. The good news is that even small wins can boost inner work life tremendously."[26] Small, incremental, and consistent steps forward have a significant impact on people's motivation. The LPI data strongly confirms this assertion by demonstrating a strong positive relationship between how often individuals were reported by their peers as identifying "measurable milestones that keep projects moving forward" and the level of motivation that peers reported. The percentage of colleagues and co-workers who indicate they are highly motivated is more than 40 times higher when working with individuals in the top quintile of identifying milestones and keeping projects moving forward, compared with those who work alongside individuals who are in the bottom quintile of this leadership behavior.

The principle of small wins doesn't just apply to organizational innovation. It can apply to improving the appearance of a city street, or adopting a new process for serving customers, or teaching kids to play a sport. Here's an example of how Rayona Sharpnack took a step-by-step approach to coaching her eight-year-old daughter's softball team. On one of the first days of practice, she had everyone try to do some batting. She took a really soft, spongy ball, and tossed it to the first girl. That girl is standing maybe ten feet away, Rayona is throwing baby tosses, but the girl screams and hides her head. So Rayona says, "Hey, no problem, Suzy. Go to the back of the line. That's fine. Betsy, you step up." But Betsy does the same thing—clutches her head and screams. So Rayona realized that she needed to do something different. She went out to her car and retrieved some whiteboard markers from her briefcase. She used the markers to make smiley faces—red, black, blue, and green—on each ball. Now, when the kids would look at a ball, all they would see was a smiley face. Rayona called the girls back over. "Okay. We're going to play a different game this time," she says. "This time, your job is to name the color of the smiley face. That's all you have to do."

So they start all over again and little Suzy stands up, and Rayona tosses a ball by her. Suzy watches it all the way and goes, "Red." Next girl, Betsy, gets up there. Betsy goes, "Green." All the girls are yelling with excitement because they can identify the color of the smiley face. Now Rayona says, "Okay. Now I want you to do the same thing, only this time I want you to hold the bat on your shoulder when the ball goes by." Same level of success. Excitement continues to build. The third time through, she asks them to touch the smiley face with the bat. In the girls' first game they beat their opponents 27 to 1.[27]

Rayona took something that was initially frightening and gradually overcame the girls' fear and the lack of skill. She coached them in increments; first on how to focus on the task and then on how to execute. If you approach new and challenging tasks this way, you could have the same success as Rayona's team. If you are uncertain about the effect of some new ideas, experiment with them first. Consumer product companies do this all the time. They try out new products in select locations before launching them in all markets. They don't wait until everything is perfect, because that's the point of the test in the first place, and the window of opportunity can close very quickly. Rapid and plentiful prototyping has been shown to bring higher-quality products to the marketplace most quickly.[28]

If your colleagues can see that you are asking them to do something that they can imagine themselves doing, they will feel some assurance that they can be successful at the task. When they don't feel overwhelmed by a task, their energy goes into getting the job done instead of wondering, "How will we ever solve that problem?" By finding all the small ways that people can succeed at doing things differently (better) than they are currently, you make people want to both become and stay involved.

Learn from Mistakes   There's no denying that change and leadership involve taking risks, and with any uncertain action, there are always, at a minimum, mistakes made, setbacks experienced, and, worse yet, failures. Two of the most short-sighted clichés are "Failure is not an option" and "Get it right the first time." Both only encourage people to play it safe. The truth is that people never get it right the first time, and progress doesn't happen in a straight line upward and to the right on some chart. Sure, you should get it right every time once you get to production or delivery, but not when you're trying to do things that have never been done before. When you engage in something new and different, you make a lot of mistakes. Everyone does. That's what experimentation is all about. There are lots of trials and errors when testing new concepts, new methods, and new practices. Keep in mind, as economist and *Financial Times* columnist Tim Harford explains, "Few of our own failures are fatal. Success comes through rapidly fixing our mistakes rather than getting things right the first time."[29]

Over and over again, people in our studies of their Personal-Best Leadership Experiences tell us how mistakes, setbacks, and even failures have played a role in their successes. Without them, there would have been little to no learning, and leaders would have been unable to realize their aspirations or achieve momentous breakthroughs. Many echo the thought that the overall quality of work improves when people have a chance to be tested, and possibly even fail. Listen to how Emily Leiter explained these lessons in her Personal-Best Leadership Experience, where at 22 years of age, the youngest at her small pharmaceutical company, she was tasked with heading up an important project involving significant changes in their sales systems. She realized that ."we needed to take some risks, fail, and learn from our mistakes." The first new sales process and systems outline they initiated was a failure on several levels, the team wasn't using the process, and the problems were continuing. Emily told us that at first her "confidence took a dive," then instead of giving up and allowing the problems to continue, she said, "I would learn from my mistakes and try again." Upon reflection she realized that the sales teams did not see the value in implementing a more formalized process. So on subsequent initiatives she and the team focused on small, incremental improvements, with each one providing an opportunity to learn, revise as needed, and take another step forward. With each implementation milestone, or small win, Emily and her colleagues discussed what had worked or not and built upon those experiences as they moved forward.

Whatever the endeavor, learning is always measured as a curve and not a straight line. In fact, most innovations could be called "failures in the middle." You seldom learn in a new endeavor without making any mistakes. Consider the times when you tried to learn a new game or a new sport. Maybe it was snowboarding, surfing, tennis, bridge, poker, or esports. It's very unlikely that you got it perfect on the very first day.

Regardless of the field, studies consistently show that there is no success without the possibility of failure.[30] It's similar to what American author, entrepreneur, and humorist Mark Twain wrote: "Good decisions come from experience. Experience comes from making bad decisions."

Shilpa Shivagange clearly took this advice to heart in her first leadership experience, where she was part of a vendor evaluation process team. She said that they had "a fair share of success and failure" in various tests and experiments and described how she documented the experience: "Throughout the process I maintained a running whiteboard list, so when things didn't go as expected I tried to look back at what we did and where we went wrong and added that to the list. This helped us remember what mistake not to do going forward."

What's truly paralyzing about the "Failure is not an option" notion is that it substantially increases the pressure to never experiment or ever do anything risky. The fears and anxieties that are produced by this perspective are magnitudes greater than those experienced when the attitude is that the only way to succeed is to try. Unless you are willing to try something that you have never tried before, you won't ever know what you are capable of doing. Here's another way to think about this. Let's say you're doing something right now that you know how to do. Then someone comes along and suggests that there's a better way. Your initial reaction might be "Well, that's okay, but the way I'm now doing it works well enough, and I'm comfortable doing it this way." Fine, but you need to realize that this is not how learning, or progress, happens. You can only learn and move forward when you experiment and experience doing differently what you already know how to do well.

Better yet, consider the case when you can say to yourself, "I don't know how to do this, and I would like to be able to." There is no other choice in this instance but to learn. Telling yourself to "get it right the first time" is a ridiculous standard to set, because you won't. The real issue is how fast can you learn? How quickly can you learn from your mistakes and your failures before you get it right? Repeatedly, people in our studies told us how much mistakes and failure have been crucial to their success, both personally and professionally. Without mistakes, they wouldn't know what they could or could not do (at least at the moment).

These experiences confirm the research, which shows that the overall quality of work improves when people have a chance to fail. For example, consider this experiment a ceramics teacher carried out in his classroom.[31] At the beginning of the semester, he divided the students into two groups. He told the first group they could earn better grades by producing more pots (e.g., 30 for a B, 40 for an A), regardless of the quality. He told the second group that their grades depended solely on the quality of the pots they produced. Not surprisingly, students in the first group got right to it, producing as many pots as possible, while the second group was quite careful and deliberate in how they went about making the best pots.

Initially, to his surprise, the teacher found that the students who made the most pots—those graded on quantity rather than quality—also made the best ones. It turned out that the practice of making lots of pots naturally resulted in better quality; for example, these students became more familiar with the intricacies of the kiln and how various firing positions affected the aesthetics of their products. Risk taking, making mistakes, and perseverance are hallmarks of innovators and leaders. You need to promote a spirit of inquiry and openness, patience, a tolerance for error, and a framework for forgiveness.

Adopt a Learning Mindset A key takeaway from Personal-Best Leadership Experiences was not about making mistakes and experiencing setbacks and failures, although they were evident; rather, the lessons were about putting yourself in a position to learn. That doesn't happen without being willing to not only work outside your comfort zone, but also to acknowledge that, just as is common in the military and healthcare, after-action reviews are held for the purpose not of finding fault but of learning from experiences that did not go completely as planned. Often, this requires a sense of reframing the experience, to focus on learning more than the results. Consider, for example, the debriefings Navy fighter pilots have after every flying mission, including Blue Angels flying jets at 700 mph, often at 18-inch wingtip separation through hundreds of acrobatic maneuvers, where mistakes can be fatal. Experienced Naval Aviator Commander Amy Tomlinson shared with us that after every flight, pilots practice self-accountability, talking freely about what worked and what did not. But when discussing what did not go as planned, rather than listing mistakes as problems, they use the term "other" to discuss the things that went wrong and what can subsequently be highlighted as a lesson for how to do better the next time. When the after-action review is not about getting called out for making a mistake and more about getting better, defensive posture lessens and learning happens in the "other" category of experiences.

In our research we find that people who are most actively involved in learning are also the ones who engage most often in The Five Practices of Exemplary Leadership.[32] Other scholars have documented that people most engaged in learning were more likely to have started something from scratch, played a significant role in an acquisition, turned around an organizational unit, negotiated a major contract, and the like.[33] In other words, the more you are engaged in learning, the more successful you are at leading—and just about anything else.

Building your capacity to be an active learner is akin to having a growth mindset, which is the belief that people's basic qualities can be improved and strengthened through their efforts, in contrast to a fixed mindset that presumes one's qualities are inherent and carved in stone. With a growth mindset you believe that you (and other people) can learn to be better leaders, while holding a fixed mindset means that you think that no amount of training or experience is going to make people better than they already are.[34] Researchers have shown, for example, that when working on simulated business problems, individuals with fixed mindsets give up more quickly and perform more poorly than those with a growth mindset. The same applies to kids in school, athletes on the playing field, teachers in the classroom, and even partners in relationships.[35]

In our studies, those with a growth mindset were more willing than those with a fixed mindset to embrace challenges, persist when facing obstacles, and sustain efforts, even when confronted with resistance. Believing that people can change and grow, growth-minded individuals were willing to foster innovation and focus on learning from setbacks. They showed a greater propensity to support experimentation by others. People with a fixed mindset avoided challenging situations and were unlikely to open themselves up to feedback of any sort.[36] Mindsets, and not skill sets, make the critical difference in deciding to take on challenging situations.

To develop a growth mindset and to nourish it in others, you need to embrace the challenges you face. That's where the learning is. When you believe that you can continuously learn, you will. Only those who believe that they can get better make an effort to do so. When you encounter setbacks—and there will be many—you have to persist. Leaders don't give up easily on themselves or others, and when things don't work out as expected, you need to view the outcome as temporary, local, and changeable. "What can be learned from this experience?" is the mantra associated with exemplary leadership, rather than "Who can be blamed?" The more frequently that individuals were reported by their peers as "Asking 'What can we learn?' when things don't go as expected," the more their colleagues assessed them as effective leaders. For those who only observed the individual engaging in this leadership behavior sometimes or less, only 11 percent strongly agreed that these individuals were effective leaders. Sixty-one percent of their peers gave the highest evaluations to those individuals who very frequently engaged in focusing on the learning and not simply the outcome.

Be Resilient   Uncertainty and risk come along with any effort to make matters better and improve upon the status quo. What's critical is how you respond to and cope with the inevitable mistakes, setbacks, failures, and accompanying stress associated with leadership.[37] For leaders, it is more about bouncing forward than simply bouncing back. Also important is how you help others handle the stress of change. Researchers have found that highly resilient employees miss fewer workdays, report higher job satisfaction, stay on the job longer, and are in better health than those unable to cope effectively with stress caused by challenge and uncertainty.[38]

The Personal-Best Leadership Experiences are all clear examples of difficult, stressful projects that generated enthusiasm and enjoyment.

Instead of being debilitated, people reported that the challenging experi-ence energized them. This internal feeling is precisely what researchers refer to as "grit."[39] Grit is an individual's ability to maintain passion and perseverance for a purpose despite a lack of positive feedback. In our research, we found a significant positive relationship between individu-als' levels of grit and how often they reported using the leadership behav-iors associated with Challenge the Process.[40] This relationship between grit and leadership was not affected by the individual's gender, age, educational level, ethnicity, or nationality. Grittiness will make you more willing to take risks and more open to learning from experience.

The ability to grow and thrive under stressful, risk-abundant situa-tions is highly dependent on how you view change. Psychologists have reported, for example, that people who experience a high degree of stress and yet cope with it positively have a distinctive attitude toward stress, which they call "psychological hardiness."[41] Researchers have found—in groups as diverse as corporate managers, entrepreneurs, students, nurses, lawyers, working professionals, artists, combat soldiers, and others—that those high in psychological hardiness are much more likely to withstand serious challenges and bounce back from failure than those low in hardi-ness.[42] It isn't the stress of uncertainty and challenge that makes people ill, it is how they respond to stressful events. The good news is that hardiness is an attitude that you can learn and strengthen.

The three key beliefs to being psychologically hardy are commit-ment, control, and challenge. To turn adversity into advantage, you first need to commit yourself to whatever is happening. You have to be involved, engaged, and curious. You can't sit back and wait for something to happen. When you commit, you find in whatever you are doing some-thing that seems interesting, meaningful, or worthwhile. You also have to take control of your own life. You need to attempt to influence what is going on. While all your attempts may not be successful, you can't sink into powerlessness or passivity or feel like a victim. Nor can you engage in denial or feel disengaged, bored, and empty. Finally, if you are going to be psychologically hardy, you need to view challenge as an opportunity to learn from both negative and positive experiences. You can't play it safe. Personal improvement and fulfillment come through the continual process of getting engaged in the uncertainties of life.

During the 2020 coronavirus pandemic lockdown, it was evident that those who handled the crisis the best were examples of how resilient individuals respond to adversity. They were able to maintain hope and find meaning and a larger purpose in the various individual changes required, despite the unfortunate pain, loss, and suffering. They made a personal commitment to do something, even something very small, to take control of what they could. They volunteered to help others, shifted their small businesses to serve a need for food or equipment, picked up groceries for the most vulnerable, or found ways to express appreciation to caregivers and first-responders.[43]

Tiffany Henderson started her job at a computer software company with the title "front office coordinator," which is also known as "receptionist." A problem-solver by nature, Tiffany approached her job with a commitment to "work on any issue that needs resolution" and a sense of control in "maintaining the viewpoint that every problem has a solution." Moreover, Tiffany loves a challenge. For instance, at the annual company summer picnic, when only one of two scheduled food trucks arrived, rather than panic, she thought, "Let's just take care of the problem," and ordered pizzas to make up for the absent truck.[44] Tiffany saw the situation as a challenge, became involved immediately in dealing with it, and took control of the situation. This is what being psychologically hardy is all about.

When efforts and plans don't turn out as expected, and unexpected circumstances arise, you can help yourself and your colleagues to cope more effectively by generating conditions under which commitment rather than alienation can be experienced, people can take control rather than feeling powerlessness, and the challenge can be seen more as an opportunity for greatness than a threat to the status quo. No one produces excellence when feeling uninvolved, insignificant, and threatened. When you get people to think about their best, they become biased in the direction of hardiness and resilience.

Take Action to Challenge the Process

The quest for change is a journey through uncharted territory. That quest tests your skills and abilities and can bring forth talents that have been dormant, undeveloped, or even unimagined. Challenge is the training ground for leadership. Exemplary leaders, therefore, search for opportunities to make a difference—even when those opportunities are sometimes thrust upon them rather than chosen. You need to remain diligent for anything that lulls you, your team, program, department, or community into a false sense of security. You need to be out in front of change, not behind it trying to catch up. The focus of your attention should be less on the routine operations and much more on the untested and untried. Continually invite and create new initiatives. Ask, "What's new? What's next? What's better?" That's where the future is.

Be willing to experiment and learn from your mistakes and setbacks. Identify and remove self-imposed constraints and organizational conventions that block innovation and creativity. Because innovation is always risky, create psychological safety and appreciate failure as a fact of experimental life. Instead of punishing it, encourage it; instead of trying to fix blame for mistakes, learn from them; instead of adding rules, promote flexibility. Embrace continuous improvement and lifelong learning.

Develop a hardy attitude about change. Venture outside the constraints of your normal routines and experiment with creative possibilities. Foster climates in which you and your colleagues alike can accept the challenge of becoming better. By having and fostering an attitude of psychological hardiness, you can turn any potential turmoil and stress of innovation and change into an adventure. Set the stage by getting started, taking the first step, and creating small wins.

In the next chapter we explain how you make it possible for people to work together in trusting relationships We will explore how you Enable Others to Act by fostering collaboration and strengthening others.

Here are two recommended actions that you should take to continuously strengthen your competence in the leadership practice of Challenge the Process:

Search for Opportunities. You probably appreciate that innovation is important and that trying new things can lead to unexpected successes. As you keep challenging yourself and your colleagues, remember that transformative ideas can come from anybody and anywhere. Reach out and make sure you're discussing challenges with a wide variety of people with different backgrounds, specialties, and viewpoints. More and better ideas come from gathering diverse ways of thinking. Make sure you are inclusive when looking for new ways of doing things and reach outside your group to see what people in other areas of your organization have to say. Ask yourself questions like, "Who could give us a new perspective on this?" and "Where can I look for feedback that I haven't looked before?" to pursue perspectives outside your immediate group.

Experiment and Take Risks. If people around you think "If it ain't broke, don't fix it," you need to flip the script. Things don't have to be broken before you "fix" them. Good judgment comes from experience, and experience is the result of making mistakes and learning from them. Transform the mindset by initiating conversations with the people you work with to discuss what is going right, what isn't working as well as it could be, and what can been done differently going forward. Because mistakes and setbacks can often be difficult to discuss, remind your colleagues that the purpose of discussing failure is *only* to learn and grow—not to blame and recriminate. In the midst of any experiment, keep everyone focused on the small wins and the progress that is being made forward.

Enable
Others to Act

CHAPTER 5

Enable Others to Act

AS A TECHNICAL analyst, Kyle Barnes was used to chaos—he was often assigned unwieldy projects that had scheduling, quality, and/or cost issues. When he started working at a large retail IT organization, he was assigned to work on a big rebranding project, involving various teams across the business. According to Kyle, the project had a "nearly impossible deadline, a backlog of unaddressed issues, and a lack of process clarity." Morale was low, as the teams involved were still recovering from previous failures and the project faced significant implementation challenges.

Although Kyle was not in any official leadership role, he quickly realized the most urgent need was to create unity among the various stakeholders. Strained and distrustful relationships between the IT team and key business partners existed, and previous unsavory experiences with projects of this sort had created a high-pressure, unenthusiastic working environment. "The lack of organization prior to this project caused a loss of trust between the Business and IT teams, resulting in hesitation to close projects until every defect was fixed and every enhancement delivered," Kyle told us. The lack of best practices and tools had also been a major factor in the teams spinning their wheels. Kyle brought to the project knowledge about a "release management" system that provided a process that would significantly assist with planning, scheduling, and organizing. His leadership challenge was getting everyone on board and working together with this system: "In taking up the challenge I saw both a need, as well as an opportunity," he said. "The teams were given a difficult task without understanding that there was a whole best-practice approach, as well as supporting processes and tools that could help them be successful."

Kyle knew that he had no direct authority to just walk into a meeting and start telling people what to do. He realized he had to first get the teams to trust one another and establish productive working relationships. Doing so would necessitate building their competence and confidence in how they could use and benefit from the new systematic approach. Knowing that his colleagues on the IT team shared a desire for things to run more smoothly and achieve successful project implementation, he started a series of conversations with that group. Then, to gain the trust of the business partners and the other project teams, Kyle took time to educate them on the system's methods and benefits. With everyone he shared organized post-project release implementation plans and kept communication and transparency levels incredibly high.

Once the project team was able to begin implementing multiple releases successfully, it was evident that the new processes and tools were indeed making a difference. His colleagues gained confidence that there were indeed better ways to organize the rebranding project, and they found ways to collaborate that they hadn't previously appreciated. "When these folks were united around a common practice," Kyle said, "everyone's confidence soared, as people felt more secure about their place in the company and within their own teams as a result of having clarified roles and responsibilities." In building up his colleagues' competence and confidence, Kyle was able to strengthen relationships to realize a significant business impact.[1]

Kyle's experience is a good illustration of something that all exemplary leaders know: Leadership is not a solo pursuit. It's a team effort. In the thousands of leadership cases we've studied, there is yet to be a single example of leadership that's occurred without the leader actively involving and relying upon the support and contributions of other people. Likewise, there hasn't been a single instance where creating competition between group members was the way to achieve the highest levels of performance. Quite the contrary, when at their personal-best as leaders, people speak passionately about teamwork and cooperation as the interpersonal route to success, especially when the conditions are extremely challenging and urgent. They understand a fundamental leadership challenge is creating an environment in which people on their team, in the department, or with the program can do their work collaboratively. These leaders know that for others to perform at their best, they need to boost everyone's competence and confidence and facilitate relationships built around trust.

The most effective leaders are those who most frequently engage in the Enable Others to Act leadership practice. Individuals asked their colleagues to complete the LPI–Observer, indicating how often they observed that person engaging in the six leadership behaviors associated with Enable Others to Act. Peers were also asked for an assessment of how effective they found this individual to be as a leader. The statistical analysis showed that effectiveness evaluations increased systematically as peers indicated this individual engaging more and more frequently in these leadership behaviors.

Foster Collaboration and Build Trust

Trust is *the* central issue in human relationships, both within and outside organizations. Without trust, you cannot lead. Individuals who are unable to trust others fail to become leaders precisely because they can't stand being dependent on the words and work of others. So they either end up doing all the work themselves, or they supervise work so closely that they become overcontrolling micromanagers. Since they don't trust other people, the result is that those people don't trust them either.

Psychologists find that individuals who are capable of trusting people are happier and more psychologically adjusted than are those who view the world with suspicion and distrust.[2] Trusting individuals are liked more by their peers and often sought out as friends. You listen more to those you trust and more readily accept their influence. The most effective leadership situations are those in which each member of the team trusts the leader, as well as one another. When Rachel Salata was put in charge of her employer's healthcare organization's nonprofit organization's annual health fair, she quickly realized that, while none of the employees who helped with the fair reported to her in any official capacity, she had to "build trust and respect by giving trust and respect." Rachel described how, with the two core employees with whom she worked the most closely, it was precisely "because we equally trusted each other and felt comfortable being honest about feedback, suggestions, or criticisms, we were able to easily bounce ideas around, have disagreements, digest our differing opinions, and come to reasonable conclusions."

Picture the people on your team and imagine that they are involved in a role-playing exercise for a research project. Each person is given identical factual information about a tough policy decision (such as budget cuts), and then they are asked as a group to solve a problem related to that information. Half of the groups involved in this study are briefed to expect trusting behavior. They are told, "You have learned from your past experiences that you can trust the other members in your group and can openly express feelings and differences with them." The other half of the groups are primed to expect just the opposite. They are prepared to expect untrusting behavior. How would the interactions play out within each of the teams? Would it surprise you to learn there were substantial differences in the ways the members of these two groups interacted and problem-solved with one another in the research?

Studies such as this one consistently show that the group members who were told they could trust their role-playing peers and manager reported their discussion and decisions were significantly more positive on *every* factor measured than were the members of the low-trust group. Members of the high-trust group were more open about their feelings, experienced greater clarity about the group's problems and goals, and searched for more alternative courses of action. They also reported having more influence on outcomes, satisfaction with the meeting, motivation to implement decisions, and closeness as a team as a result of the meeting.[3]

It's crucial to keep in mind that these were *simulations*. They actually happened, but the participants were role playing! People behaved and responded the way they did as a consequence of being *told* that they couldn't trust one another. Their actions demonstrated that trust or distrust can come with a mere suggestion—and in mere minutes. Believing that one can trust others is a significant predictor of how people will behave and how satisfied they will be with their organizations.

You show people that you trust them when you listen, provide opportunities for them to contribute freely, make choices, and be innovative. You demonstrate trust when you nurture openness, involvement, personal satisfaction, and high levels of commitment to excellence. Knowing that trust is essential, make sure that you consider alternative viewpoints, draw upon other people's expertise and abilities, and let others exercise influence over group decisions. Such actions confirm people's belief that they can rely on you to do what's in everyone's best interests.

While trust is a reciprocal process, the responsibility for anteing up first rests with you. When you say, "Trust me" but don't by your actions demonstrate that you trust others, or take the time to listen and be open to being influenced, then trust doesn't blossom or flourish. Trust begets trust. The truth is that trust comes first; following comes second. The feeling of "we" cannot happen without trust.

Show Concern for Others   Showing concern for others is one of the clearest and most unambiguous signals of your trustworthiness. When others know you will put their interests ahead of your own, they won't hesitate to trust you.[4] However, this is something people need to see in your actions—actions such as listening, paying attention to their ideas and concerns, helping them solve their problems, and being open to their influence. When you show your openness to their ideas and your interest in their concerns, people will be more open to yours. For example, Abey Mukkanachery, product operations specialist with a health and measurement company, told us about how one of his colleagues was tasked with writing specifications for a new project. "That team member felt overwhelmed with all the work that was required for this project," Abey said, "and I felt that as a teammate I should reach out and help. I approached my colleague and offered my assistance. In turn, other teammates also felt encouraged to reach out and help. We all ended up making contributions to implementing the new process for project requirements." Demonstrating empathy goes a long way in illustrating that you are concerned with more than your own interests.

Listening and attending to the needs of others are central to demonstrating empathy. You need to see the world through others' eyes and make sure that you consider alternative viewpoints. You demonstrate empathy when you volunteer to collaborate with people who are having difficulties completing an assignment, when you arrive early to greet everyone and inquire about how they are doing, and when you take the time to coach people who are taking on new jobs and responsibilities. Showing interest in others, being sensitive to their problems, and conveying compassion increases peoples' capacities to do their jobs. Your colleagues have to feel that they can talk freely with you about their challenges. To be open to sharing their ideas, their frustrations, and their dreams, they have to believe that you'll be caring and constructive in your responses. They have to feel, like Abey's colleague did, that you care about their best interests. A common refrain about what people said they would share with other people based on their own Personal-Best Leadership Experience was: "You have to understand how others feel and determine what you can do to help others to be successful. You should want to be remembered for how you served others and not as the one being served."

When people believe that you have their interests at heart—that you care about them—they're more likely to be open to your influence. It is also true that the more people feel you listen to them, and understand their feelings and perspectives, the more favorable they will feel about their relationship with you. Consider the empirical relationship found between the extent to which peers indicated that one of their colleagues actively listens to diverse points of view and also how they felt about their workplace. LPI data showed a strong relationship between colleagues' ratings of how frequently the individual listened and how strongly they believed that the individual brought out the best of people's talents and abilities, as shown in Figure 5. A similarly dramatic relationship was found between actively listening and the extent to which peers felt valued by this person, and also how much they experienced a strong sense of team spirit.

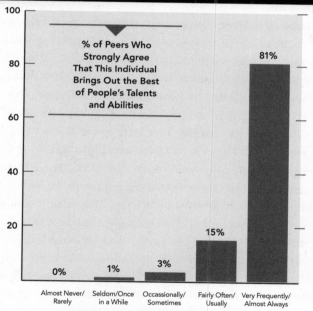

Figure 5 Bring Out the Best of People's Talents and Abilities by Listening to Diverse Viewpoints

Active listening involves more than simply paying attention. The best listeners, according to a study involving nearly 3,500 participants in a coaching skills development program, did much more than remain silent while the other person talked.[5] They demonstrated that they were listening by asking questions that "promoted discovery and insight." At its best, active listening is like having a conversation. It requires more than just hearing the other person's words. It means being engaged in a way that makes the conversation a positive experience, causing the person to whom you are listening to feel supported and valued. Showing appreciation for others' unique viewpoints demonstrates respect for them and their ideas. Being sensitive to what others are going through creates bonds that make it easier to accept one another's guidance and advice. Great listeners also tend to offer suggestions and have been described as "trampolines" in that you feel you can bounce ideas off of them.[6] Having the best interests of those around you builds trusting relationships and is facilitated by positive interdependence.

Facilitate Positive Interdependence and Reciprocity

One of the most significant ingredients to cooperation and collaboration is a sense of interdependence, a condition by which people know that they cannot succeed unless everyone else succeeds, or at least that they cannot succeed unless they coordinate their efforts. If there's no sense that "we're all in this together," that the success of one depends on the success of the other, then it's virtually impossible to create the conditions for positive teamwork. The motivation for working diligently on your own job, keeping in mind the overall common objective, is reinforced when it is the end-result that gets rewarded and not merely individual efforts.

This was precisely the situation Mayank Bhatnagar described in his Personal-Best Leadership Experience. Over the holidays, from Christmas through New Year's, he and two people from different functions "were essentially forced to work as a team on this project" at a small optical sensor startup company. However, he said that as they worked with one another, they got to know each other better and "communications became seamless as we grew together and learned what all we needed from each other to see the project through." To make extraordinary things happen, people have to rely on each other. No matter your role or position on the team, you have to take an active role in creating both a positive context and structure for cooperation and collaboration. As Mayank reported, "It was easy to get cooperation from team members because we shared ownership, each of us wanted to see the project succeed, and complete the task as quickly as possible."

Over 80 percent of colleagues and co-workers in the LPI data reported that they experienced a strong sense of team spirit when their colleagues very frequently developed "cooperative relationships among the people they work with." This is because collaboration results from people understanding that they have to rely and depend upon one another for their mutual success. A collective purpose binds people into cooperative efforts. Shared values and visions serve this function for the long term, and group goals provide this same common focus for the shorter term. Only through shared goals and recognized interdependence in one another's success can people diligently strive to create integrative solutions. Asking for help and sharing information comes naturally when people realize that they can depend on others to collaborate. When people see themselves in a mutually beneficial relationship, they have little trouble finding and setting a common goal. Make sure that the people you are working with understand the goal they are working toward, feel a shared stake in the outcome, have an appreciation for the talents and resources people bring to the endeavor, and have the latitude necessary to be both imaginative and strategic.

Also essential to developing cooperative relationships is a norm of reciprocity. The power of reciprocity is dramatically demonstrated in a well-known series of studies involving the Prisoner's Dilemma.[7] Two parties (individuals or groups) are confronted with a series of situations in which they must decide whether or not to cooperate. They don't know in advance how the other party will behave. There are two basic strategies— cooperate (don't say anything) or compete (blame the other party)—and four possible outcomes based on the choices players make—win-lose, lose-win, lose-lose, and win-win.

The maximum individual payoff comes when one player selects a noncooperative strategy and the other player chooses to cooperate in good faith. In this "I win, but you lose" approach, one party gains at the other's expense. Although this might seem to be the most successful strategy—at least for the noncooperative player—it rarely proves to be successful in the long run, mainly because the other player won't continue to cooperate in the face of the first player's noncooperative strategy. This typically leads to both parties deciding not to cooperate and attempting to maximize their respective individual payoffs, resulting in the end that both lose. However, when both parties choose to cooperate, both win, though in the short run the personal payoff for a cooperative move (win-win) is less than what it might be for a competitive one (win-lose).

Over the years researchers have found, amazingly enough, that when faced with such predicaments, the most successful strategy, in the long run, is quite simple: cooperate on the first move and then do whatever the other player did on the previous move. This strategy succeeds by eliciting cooperation from others, not by defeating them.[8] It demonstrates both a willingness to be cooperative and an unwillingness to be taken advantage of. As a long-term strategy, reciprocity minimizes the risk of escalation: if people know that you'll respond in kind, why would they start trouble? Your colleagues learn that the best way to deal with you is to cooperate and become recipients of your cooperation.

Simply put, people who reciprocate are more likely to be successful than those who try to maximize individual advantage. Drawing on surveys and performance records, researchers found that those engineers who maintained equal and reciprocal exchanges with their colleagues were not only the most productive members of their organization but also considered the most trustworthy.[9] This meant that more people listened to them and were willing to help them.

Reciprocity leads to predictability and stability in relationships; in other words, trust. It's less stressful to work with others when you understand how they will behave in response, which keeps both relationships and negotiations from breaking down.[10] Treat others as you would like for them to treat you, and it is likely they will repay you many times over. In addition, once you help others to succeed, acknowledge their accomplishments, and let them shine; they will never forget it. Whether the rewards of cooperation are tangible or intangible, when people understand that they will be better off by cooperating, they're inclined to recognize the legitimacy of others' interests in an effort to promote their own welfare.

Be More Giving   If one party always gives and the other always takes, the one who gives will feel taken advantage of, and the one who takes will feel superior. In that climate, collaboration is virtually impossible. Researchers have consistently found that organizations filled with "givers"—people who help others—are consistently more effective than those loaded with "takers." Knowing about the amount of help people are willing to give one another is a highly accurate predictor of a team's effectiveness.[11] In a series of studies, teams were rewarded for being the highest-performing team as a whole, prompting members to work together as givers. In contrast, a taker-culture was prompted in teams in which the rewards went to the highest-performing individual within each team. While the competitive teams finished their tasks faster than the cooperative teams, they were less accurate, often simply because members withheld critical information from each other.[12]

To boost the accuracy of the competitive teams, the researchers next had them complete a second task under the giving structure. That is, this time around they rewarded the entire team for high performance. Unfortunately, neither accuracy nor speed went up, and the reason was because people struggled to transition from competition to cooperation—that is, from being takers to being givers. It appears that once people had experienced their colleagues as competitors, they were no longer able to believe they could trust them. Completing even a single task under a structure that rewarded taking was enough to create win–lose mindsets, and these persisted even after the structure was removed.

Cooperative behavior requires people to understand that by working together they will be able to accomplish something that no one can accomplish alone. You wouldn't necessarily think of fencing as a team sport, but that's what nationally ranked fencing champion Zachary Chien worked on getting the students he coached to realize in their practice sessions. He said that his most difficult challenge "was creating an environment that fostered collaboration amongst all my students because, at the end of the day, fencing is an individual sport, so athletes often prioritized their own development."

The fencers tended to be quite competitive and didn't socialize and bond as much as athletes in other team sports. To fix this, Zach created skill games and drills that required "giving." For example, students would fence each other, and after each touch, whoever scored needed to tell the partner exactly how the point was set up. Zach found that once the fencers began showing more support toward one another he was able to get them to buy into the larger idea that fostering collaboration and sharing growth was in everyone's best interest: "I told them that they couldn't get to the top on their own, and I alone couldn't help get them there. They needed the support from the people they practice with. In order to be the best, you have to beat the best."

Figuring out how to take as much as possible from others—while contributing as little as possible—does not create greatness. You need to make sure that the long-term benefits of working together and giving are greater than the short-term benefits of working alone or competing with others on your team. You need to get people to realize that by working together they can complete the project faster than by focusing on short-term individual victories resulting from doing their own thing, complaining, blaming, or contending with others for scarce resources.

Maintain Durable Social Connections   The new currency of the Internet Age and the IoE (internet of everything) is not intellectual capital; it is *social capital*—the collective value of the people you know and what you will do for each other. When social connections are strong and numerous, there's more trust, reciprocity, information flow, collective action, and elevated well-being. Having strong social relationships is the best predictor of human happiness, trumping wealth, income, and material possessions; and those who fail to achieve this most basic need experience loneliness, anxiety, depression, low self-esteem, obesity, and anger.[13] You need to find ways to get connected to the information, resources, and influence you will need to make a difference. In doing so, figure out substantive ways to connect your colleagues with one another and with those outside the boundary of your group or team who are part of other key networks.

The importance of social connections has been dramatically illustrated during the COVID-19 pandemic. While nearly everyone around the world was ordered to maintain "physical distance," the yearning for social *connection* increased. People invented all kinds of ways to continue to interact with their fellow human beings. Virtual coffee breaks and cocktail hours popped up immediately after people had to shelter in place.

Residents stood on their balconies and sang to each other. Friends and family organized drive-by birthday and graduation celebrations. The demand for virtual gathering services nearly broke the Internet. There was seemingly no end to the creative ways that people invented to stay connected to each other, even in the worst of the crisis.

The most well-connected individuals are typically those who are involved in activities outside of their immediate job function or discipline, and who avoid being too strongly typecast in one field, function, administrative body, or community. Find ways to meet people from a wide range of units, departments, projects, and professions. While specialization has its benefits, from a leadership perspective you don't want to get stuck in a rut. If your connections are only in your specialty, you will be less influential than if your connections cross a lot of boundaries. When it comes to social connections, there's a payoff in mining deep and wide.

Greater connectedness can also be fostered when you and your colleagues have enough confidence in one another's relationships to ask for help when needed. The impulse to give help when requested is a powerful, automatic, and emotional response formed early in life.[14] However, in many situations people underestimate how willing others would be to provide assistance when requested. There is a social cost to saying "no" when someone asks for help. The person can be seen as uncaring, unreasonable, insensitive, and even cruel. Saying "yes," by contrast, is a more positive and rewarding experience, and agreeing to help or cooperate strengthens the bond of connectedness between people. By making someone else happy, the person who has agreed to help also feels good about himself or herself and strengthens the bond of connectedness between them. Researchers have demonstrated that people underestimate by nearly 50 percent the likelihood of receiving a positive response when requesting assistance, and this leads to lost opportunities, like prospective friends, colleagues, and clients going uncontacted, and squandering chances to increase connectedness.[15] When you feel a sense of connection with someone else, you are more likely to volunteer your assistance, as is often demonstrated by onlookers who are most predisposed to help emergency victims if they feel they share something with them.

Feeling connected to the people you are working with enhances feelings of well-being and fosters greater commitment to colleagues. Research documents that high-quality connections contribute to people flourishing, resulting in better health, higher cognitive functioning, broader thinking, and stronger resilience.[16] Individuals with high-quality relationships also have a better sense of whom to trust and not trust. They are more open, and they more fully understand themselves and the viewpoints of others.

You can more effectively develop your leadership abilities by connecting to people who can teach you about the skills you would like to acquire and the things you would like to achieve. Find out about their struggles, hardships, and mistakes as well as their accomplishments. Consider connecting with people who are not particularly well known but who nonetheless exhibit deep competence, unswerving dedication, and a good sense of who they are. Most importantly, select people who make you feel good about yourself. After all, the purpose of these relationships is to encourage and inspire you to be your best version of yourself. Travis Carrigan, a senior engineer, told us that he's been doing exactly this for years, which has led to some great opportunities and collaborative work. "These relationships," he says, "are phenomenal at helping me become a better leader, listener, and engineer."

What about *virtual* connections? Aren't they a good way to foster collaboration and build trust? There is no question that virtual connections are prolific, and in a global economy no organization could function if people had to fly halfway around the world to exchange information, make decisions, or resolve disputes. Proof of this can be found with the exponential growth in virtual communications during the global COVID-19 pandemic, and that demand has led to the development of new apps and platforms to meet the need. With a large percentage of people working from home and almost all educational institutions' classes going online, virtual connections became the most frequent way in which people communicated, learned, and conducted business.

That said, the stroke of a key, the click of a mouse, or the switch of a video doesn't get you the same results that an in-person conversation does. In an era that is becoming more and more dependent on virtual connections, there's a temptation to believe that such connections automatically lead to better relationships and greater trust. Unfortunately, virtual trust is much more difficult to both build and maintain than is trust developed in-person. Even among Gen Z employees, who make up 20 percent of today's workforce, 72 percent indicate they prefer face-to-face communication at work.[17]

Virtual trust, like virtual reality, is still one step removed from the real thing. People are social animals; it is their nature to want to interact face-to-face.[18] Bits and bytes and pixilated images make for a very fragile social foundation. As handy as virtual tools such as email, voice mail, apps, and texts are for staying in touch, they are no substitute for positive face-to-face interactions. If you mainly know the members of your group virtually, you probably do not know them well enough to trust them with extremely important matters. This may sound heretical in a world driving itself more and more to depend on electronic connections, but you have to figure out how to combine and balance the benefits of technology with the social imperative of human contact. Data and information may be virtually shared, but ensuring understanding, sensitivity, knowledge, and action online or at a distance are kinks still to be worked out.

In order to cement your social capital, you have to intensify the durable nature of relationships. People who like being in the relationship and expect their interactions to continue into the future—for example, they'll run into one another at some event, continue to serve on this project team for several years, or participate in a subsequent task force—are much more likely to cooperate in the here-and-now. Knowing that you have to deal with someone again, whether tomorrow, next week, or in the foreseeable future, ensures that you will not easily forget how you've treated one another. When interactions are likely to be frequent, the consequences of today's actions on tomorrow's dealings are that much more pronounced. In the end, enduring relationships, more than one-time or short-term ones, provide incentives to find ways to work together cooperatively to ensure mutual success in the future.

Strengthen Others

It is paradoxical, but the most effective leaders are those who give their power away to others. That is, they make those around them feel strong and capable. They listen to and credit others' ideas, and they make sure that people do not feel left out of the loop when it comes to important decisions. They help their colleagues take ownership and feel a sense of responsibility for achievements. They enhance the competence and self-confidence of those around them.

Feeling powerful—literally, feeling "able"—comes from a deep sense of being in control of life. People everywhere share this inclination. When they feel capable of determining their destiny, and when they believe they can mobilize the resources and support necessary to complete a task, then they are better able to persist in their efforts to achieve. But when people feel controlled by others, when they believe they are unsupported, or lack the necessary resources, they show little to no commitment to excel (although they may still have to comply). When you increase another's sense of self-confidence, which makes that individual feel more powerful, you greatly enhance the energy and effort he or she will devote to being effective. Gallup surveys, involving millions of people around the world, decidedly show a close link between how powerful and engaged people feel in their workplace and productivity, commitment, and retention.[19]

Traditional thinking promotes the archaic idea that power is a fixed sum, and correspondingly, if you give any of your power away to others, you will have less power and be less powerful. Not surprisingly, people with this view hold tightly to the power that they perceive is theirs and are extremely reluctant to share it. This notion is wrongheaded and inconsistent with all the evidence on high-performing organizations. When you give some responsibility to others, they become invested and passionate about the assignment. You are not so much giving your power away as you are providing an opportunity for people to use the "power" that they already have to create, to make decisions, and to feel that they have control over what they are doing. Researchers have found that organizational effectiveness and member satisfaction follow from people believing that they have some degree of influence and control in their organization. Shared power results in higher job fulfillment and performance throughout the organization.[20]

These workplace lessons resonate with Karyn DeMartini's Personal-Best Leadership Experience, which involved 14 members of her extended family as they dealt with their aunt Lala's illness. Karyn's story began with an acknowledgment that her family did not deal very well with crisis. "We're stubborn, hotheaded, set in our ways, resistant to change—far from any 'poster-family' of how to communicate in a healthy fashion," she said. The situation would require them to pull together as a family like they had never had to before. Beyond the normal routines of life and work, there were many tasks and details that needed attending to, including driving Lala to various doctors' appointments, cooking meals, talking with healthcare specialists, and communicating information about Lala's condition to other family members—in nine different locations. There was also enlisting in support groups, paying bills, and working with insurance providers. Karyn soon learned the importance of giving power away. As she explained:

> I have historically tried to control most facets of other projects I have worked on. In this situation, however, I truly learned the importance of looking at leadership as a relationship. The task of giving my power away and asking certain relatives to take charge of specific projects (e.g., a particular doctor appointment) was easier than I expected. Family members felt needed and empowered. They felt like they were making a positive impact on a terrible situation. I always thought people hated receiving more work, so to speak, but I now realize that projects are valued and welcomed if the work is important to the receiver.
>
> Many of my family members had important insights and creative ideas that I had not seen. Giving my power away by encouraging others to take charge helped our family to deal with these issues in a new and beneficial manner. Now that I

see the benefits of giving my power away, I do this even
sooner—in my family and in my workplace. As new dilemmas
and challenges surface, I make more of a conscious effort to
encourage people to get involved or carry out ideas
they develop.

As Karyn learned, when you make other people feel powerful, in
tangible and/or intangible ways, you are demonstrating profound trust in
and respect for their abilities. When you help others grow and develop,
the assistance and support you provide are likely to be reciprocated. Such
actions also serve to reinforce people accepting accountability for both
their actions and results and they strengthen others' resolve not to let
your trust and faith in them dissipate.

Provide Choices   Freedom is the ability to make choices. *Trapped*
is the word that people generally use when they believe that they do not
have any latitude about how they can behave. When people feel trapped,
they often act as rats caught in a maze; believing they have no alternatives,
they typically stop moving and eventually shut down. Amanda Itilong
gave voice to these feelings as she described her experience in the process
of getting cancer scans. She observed one radiology tech come out to
greet patients for a CT scan with a contrast drink already prepared.
"This might sound efficient," Amanda said, "but as a patient it's really
frustrating if you don't get a personal choice of the flavor of the drink.
It gets worse when a few minutes later a different radiology tech comes
out and gives her patient five different flavor choices for contrast. So my
tech just picked a random flavor for me and didn't even tell me there were
choices?" Amanda's poignant observation that "patients need choices to
feel like they have a little control in their healthcare experience, where
they're usually without much control," is just as relevant and applicable
in a work, community, or any other setting. People need to feel in control
of their own lives, and you should do what you can to ensure that they
have choices.

Being able to have a choice, and the ability to exercise a choice, that
is, having a sense of genuine autonomy, makes people feel powerful and

increases their willingness to exercise their capabilities more fully. Researchers at the Delgado Lab for Social and Affective Neuroscience at Rutgers University report that the perception of increased choice activates reward-related circuits in the brain, which makes people feel more at ease, enhancing their willingness to experiment and venture outside of their comfort zones.[21]

High-performing organizations result from people's willingness to work beyond their job descriptions, and this happens because they have the latitude and discretion to make choices about both the work they do and how they do it. In the LPI data the individual's peers were asked about the extent to which they felt this person provided them with "a great deal of freedom and choice in deciding how to do their work." How proud they were to tell others they work for the organization was strongly related to this leadership behavior. About 5 percent strongly agreed that they felt proud when they experienced the individual providing this latitude only once in a while or less. In contrast, 90 percent strongly agreed they were proud when the individual provided freedom and choice fairly often or more.

No one wakes up in the morning and is excited to go to work so that they can be incompetent and disruptive. People want to be seen as responsible and productive, taking initiative, and being self-directed. Constantly told what to do by a leader and how to do it by some rulebook stymie these inclinations. People want to think for themselves, not continually having to ask someone, "What should I do?" Lacking freedom of choice and operating in prescribed and predetermined ways makes people unable, and even unwilling, to respond when a situation arises that is not in the script. When people have to ask the "higher-ups" what to do— even if they think they know what needs to be done and feel they can do it—the entire operation slows down. The only way to create an efficient and effective organization is by finding opportunities for people to use their best judgment in applying their knowledge and skills. Doing so is an explicit exercise in trust.

As necessary as choice is, however, it is insufficient. Without the knowledge, skills, information, and resources to do a job expertly and without feeling competent to effectively execute the choices that it requires, people can easily feel overwhelmed and fearful of making mistakes. This means making every effort to ensure that you and your colleagues are prepared to make choices and are willing to be held accountable.

Build Competence and Confidence   You cannot do what you do not know how to do. Providing increasing levels of responsibility and discretion requires an accompanying increase in training and development experiences, as well as the chance to learn on the job. In order for people to feel highly capable, they must continuously improve and develop their skills and abilities. But even if individuals know *how* to do something, it doesn't mean that they *will* do it. They may be reluctant to exercise their judgment because they lack the confidence to perform critical tasks in specific situations, fear making mistakes, or lack relevant information about the job.

Without sufficient self-confidence, people will not have the commitment required for taking on tough challenges. Diplomat and statesman Adlai Stevenson II once said, "It's hard to lead a cavalry charge if you think you look funny on a horse," and his humorous observation is supported by research. The lack of confidence manifests itself in feelings of helplessness, powerlessness, and often crippling self-doubt. In building your self-confidence, and doing the same for those around you, you are bolstering the inner strength necessary to forge ahead in uncharted terrain, to face opposition, and to make tough choices.[22]

Empirical studies document how self-confidence affects people's performance. Participants were told that decision making was a skill developed through practice. The more they worked at it, the more capable they became. The researchers told another group of participants that decision making reflected one's basic intellectual aptitude. The higher their underlying cognitive capacities, the better their decision-making ability would be. Both groups worked through a series of problems in a simulated organization. Participants who believed that decision making was an acquirable skill continued to set challenging goals for themselves, used effective problem-solving strategies, and fostered organizational productivity. Their counterparts who believed that decision-making ability was inherent—that is, you either have it, or you don't—lost confidence in themselves as they encountered difficulties. They lowered their aspirations for the task, their problem solving deteriorated, and organizational productivity declined.[23]

In reflecting back on her Personal-Best Leadership Experience, which involved major internal system changes, Karina Chamorro realized that she was initially short-sighted in thinking that the project team structure limited her ability to strengthen those around her because she was neither the project leader nor the department head. What she did come to appreciate is that she could boost not only her colleagues' competencies but their self-confidence simply by helping to ensure that responsibilities and tasks were distributed around in ways that "aligned tasks to experience and interests whenever possible." She explained: "Different colleagues led when they were best positioned to manage that situation because they felt particularly passionate about an issue or idea or were going to be impacted by a project team decision." Like Karina, you can help to identify and leverage teammate capabilities and give them opportunities to exercise leadership.

As revealed in the Personal-Best Leadership Experiences and in empirical research—and probably your own experience underscores—having confidence and believing in your ability to handle the job, no matter how difficult, is essential in promoting and sustaining consistent efforts. Fostering self-efficacy is not a warmed-over version of the power of positive thinking. You must communicate your belief that people can be successful. This sentiment was quite apparent in most people's personal-bests—someone believed in them and gave them the chance to make something extraordinary happen. Knowing that someone expected them to succeed motivated them to extend themselves, and to persevere in the face of hardships and any setbacks.

Foster Personal Responsibility and Accountability   Mykell
Bates had played soccer from the age of 14 and was chosen captain of the U.S. Under-17 national team when he was just 15 years old. When he went on to college, his soccer playing continued, and in his sophomore year Mykell

was chosen captain of the soccer team. None of the players reported to him in any formal organizational sense, and Mykell realized that since they depended upon each other on the field, why should that be any different off the field? "We all play an important part in our success on the field," he explained, "so all I was asking for was that same level of accountability and connection to the team off the field. When I'd ask a player 'Hey, can you text the guys about the team meeting tonight?' they always stepped up." Slowly Mykell began passing on responsibilities to more members of the team. Ultimately, it became clear that spreading out some of the tasks was a much more efficient way of doing things, and it helped all those who contributed feel accountable for the successful operation of the team.

What Mykell did with the team is what all leaders do to foster accountability: they consciously create an environment in which team members count on one another to do what needs to be done. This doesn't mean they are autocratic or controlling. As one of his teammates told us, "Mykell was not directive in handing out tasks; he would simply ask for your help, and you would want to help him. He trusted that I could do the job that needed to be done, and I didn't want to break that trust. It was mutual respect, for each other and for the good of the team."

Asking his soccer teammates to step up and take over some of the operational tasks for the soccer team had another benefit beyond fostering accountability. By spreading responsibilities among the group, each teammate could specialize and perfect one thing rather than having one person take it all on. A seminar participant took to heart Mykell's example, and when he came back to us several months later he told us how he had learned that giving others responsibilities enhanced their skills and self-confidence: "I have a part-time construction job, and Mykell's leadership showed me that one thing I can do is pass on some of the building responsibilities to others. I have always liked doing everything myself, but I am sure the guys I am working with can do just as well as I can, if not better in some cases. I can coach them through it, and that will build their capabilities and confidence, eventually making us a much stronger and more productive work team."

Just like Mykell, you have to appreciate a fundamental truth about strengthening others: the power to choose can only be sustained if people are willing to be held accountable. The more freedom of choice people have, the more personal responsibility they must accept. This comes with a bonus: The more that people believe that everyone is taking responsibility for his or her part of the project—and has the competence to do it—the more trusting and the more cooperative they will be. People will be more confident in doing their part when they believe others will do theirs.

Accountability is a critical element in every collaborative effort. When people take personal responsibility and hold themselves accountable for their actions, their colleagues will be considerably more inclined to work with them and be more cooperative. Everyone has to do his or her part for a group to function effectively. Personal accountability is enhanced when the situation is structured so that people have to work collaboratively with one another. Knowing that your peers are expecting you to be prepared and to do your job is a powerful force in motivating each person to do well. The feeling of not wanting to let the rest of the group down strengthens each individual's resolve to do his or her best. Additionally, the more people believe that everyone else is competent and taking responsibility for a part of the job, the more trusting and cooperative they will be. It's also true that people will be more committed to doing their part when confident that others will be doing theirs.

Facilitating self-confidence is what Mykell was doing when he started spreading around the tasks and responsibilities that traditionally had belonged to the soccer team captain. "When Mykell asked me to do something, it instilled confidence in my abilities," teammate Brandon Zimmerman told us. "When he would ask me to take on some of his day-to-day responsibilities, it gave me the confidence and competence to perform those tasks. All Mykell did was give me the authority to use the skills that he believed I already had, but maybe I wasn't acknowledging in myself. The more he did this, the more it worked to the advantage of the group as a whole, because each of us became stronger."

When you explicitly give people the freedom to make choices, you are implicitly increasing the degree of personal responsibility they must necessarily accept. The interconnectedness between choice and accountability takes on increasing importance in virtually linked global workplaces. As Mykell's experience demonstrated, fostering accountability meant delegating responsibilities and providing others with the chance to take ownership. By trusting others, he was letting them know that he believed in them and had confidence in their ability and judgment. Given the level of trust he demonstrated in them, they, in turn, felt greater motivation to follow through with their commitments. When you allow others to take on more responsibility, you also benefit by being able to take on new duties and learning opportunities yourself.

Coach and Mentor While you can communicate your confidence in others, you can't just tell people they can do something if they actually can't—yet. Coaching is essential to enabling people to be their best. A three-year study of the impact of training documented the importance of coaching as it reported how high-improvement learners were four times more likely to have had indicated that they had *coaching* conversations than individuals who showed little or no improvement.[24] In other words, improvement isn't merely about educational experiences; it's the coaching and mentoring associated with those opportunities that matters.

People often underestimate what they can learn from their peers and the people on their teams. Coaching is not a job, but a process that relies especially on an interpersonal relationship. The relationship doesn't need to be official, or even to be formally acknowledged. You can coach as a friend, colleague, or family member. It is necessary to demonstrate an interest in helping someone build competence and confidence—focusing on individual needs and engaging the person in a process of learning. As a coach, you need to understand that strengthening others requires paying deep attention to not only what others are saying and doing, but also to how they are viewed by those around them. You also need to fundamentally believe that anyone you are coaching is essentially smart enough to figure things out when given the opportunity to make choices, provided with support, and provided with meaningful and constructive feedback. Consider how Nils Hansen, a senior buyer with a multinational retailing organization, described what he did to coach his teammates to do something they had never done before: "I encouraged each team member to speak up with new ideas, ask questions, and feel empowered to make decisions. I let them know that I had confidence in their capabilities and gave them the space to trust themselves. I made it a point to remind them that they had what it took to deliver all the goals set forth before us." Coaching stretches people to grow and develop their capabilities, and it provides them with opportunities to hone and enhance their skills in both routine and challenging assignments.

Think about how you can ask good questions, regardless of your official status as a coach, because the benefits of asking questions are numerous. For one, it gives people the space to think about and to frame issues from their perspectives. Second, asking questions indicates an underlying trust in people's abilities by shifting accountability to them. Third, it has the benefit of creating almost immediate buy-in for the solution (after all, it's their idea). Questions also help to focus people's attention and thinking.

Another avenue for coaches is making connections for the people you are working with to individuals you have relationships with who can be role models they can learn from. These are people who can share invaluable lessons from their experiences. By observing exemplars, people can gain insights into the dynamic nature of the proficiency they themselves aspire to acquire. Positive role models are necessary for growth and development because no one can easily excel based on a negative. You excel best by emulating a positive example. That is, while you may know 100 things *not* to do, if you don't know even one thing *to* do, then you can't perform very well at the task. Help others take the next steps of creating a mental picture of performing relevant skills and internalizing why it is vital to develop those competencies. Seek out those people from whom you as well as others can learn.

Even coaches need coaches, so consider assembling a group of coaches for yourself by creating a personal board of directors.[25] Typically, such a board includes five to seven people (who probably will never all meet one another but have a relationship with you) who can help with your personal development. Meet with them on a one-on-one basis. Some board members may already be your "fans" (people who support you and will deliver corrective feedback with good intent), and others could be potential "sponsors" (people who can advocate for you when it's time for a new assignment or advancement). The common denominator is that they are people you can learn from. One reason for having many people on your board is that no one can teach you everything you need to know.

Whether or not you are a coach or have a coach, the central issue is that you cannot know how you are doing without asking for feedback and learning about the consequences of your actions on other people. Asking for feedback provides a perspective that only others can see, and armed with this insight you have the opportunity to make improvements. People who seek out disconfirming feedback—information that is contrary to their self-perceptions—perform better than those who only listen to people who see their positive qualities.[26] Being aware of your weaknesses and shortcomings is critical to improvement and being the best you can be.

Take Action to Enable Others to Act

"You can't do it alone" is the mantra of exemplary leaders. You can't make extraordinary things happen all by yourself. You need to foster collaboration and strengthen others.

Fostering collaboration enables departments, projects, schools, and communities to function effectively. Collaboration can be sustained only when you promote the feeling that "we're all in this together." Mutual goals and roles contribute to mutual interdependence. Knowing that people will reciprocate is the best incentive for helping others to achieve their goals. Help begets help, just as trust begets trust. Focusing on what's to be gained fosters agreement in what might otherwise be divisive issues. Create a trusting climate by the example you set. Make sure that the key people around you and in your network are able to make human contact with one another. Work to make these interactions durable and connect people to multiple sources of influence and information.

You strengthen others when you make it possible for them to exercise choice and discretion, when you develop in others the competence and confidence to act and to excel, and when you foster the accountability that compels action. Exemplary leaders use their power and influence in the service of others because they know that the best performance emanates from capable and confident people.

Here are two recommended actions that you should take to continuously strengthen your competence in the leadership practice of Enable Others to Act:

Foster Collaboration. Help begets help, just as trust begets trust, so be willing to take the initiative to lend a helping hand to those around you. Go first in establishing an expectation of reciprocity and that you will treat others not just as you would like to be treated but by how they would like to be treated. The next time you're talking with colleagues or co-workers, take the time to listen carefully and demonstrate empathy for their points of view, caring about how they feel and what they believe. Practice being an active listener because responding thoughtfully and compassionately to someone else's view significantly strengthens your working relationship. Discuss why the two (or more) of you are working together and ensure that your answers clarify the "we" in each of your objectives.

Strengthen Others. When someone is having a problem you've also experienced, share your own lessons and recommendations. If someone needs help, consider whether you can connect that person with a resource that might be useful. Let people know you have confidence in their abilities and offer your support when they are stretching themselves in untested areas. After attending workshops or seminars, bring back ideas and applications that you can share to help build the capabilities of others. Connect colleagues with intersecting interests, and give them the opportunity to share resources, learn together, and turn to each other with questions, ideas, and concerns. Facilitate mentorships; for example, by identifying co-workers who can learn from, as well as with, each other. When you partner people up, you create a built-in support structure for ongoing learning, and ultimately improve everyone's ability to grow and develop.

In the next chapter we explain how you sustain motivation and momentum along the path to success. We will explore how you Encourage the Heart by recognizing contributions and celebrating values and victories.

Encourage
the Heart

CHAPTER 6

Encourage the Heart

IN THE ACCOUNT of his Personal-Best Leadership Experience, Alex Dinh voiced issues common to many leaders without titles. "As a product manager for a line of products within my work organization," he told us, "I am often challenged with leading a cross-functional team that consists of members from engineering, marketing, operations, sales, and support, but I don't have any direct authority over them. This is inherently challenging as I am influencing team members to prioritize my requests along with those of their direct supervisors, account managers, other product managers, and even their own self-interests."

This situation was particularly frustrating for Alex because he had previously managed a team with direct reports, and he felt that he had gone out of his way to make sure that the team was recognized for their work and felt appreciated. "I was motivated to do this," he said, "since I felt responsible for their performance, career advancements, and happiness at work. Upon transitioning to an individual contributor, I no longer felt responsible for providing this type of encouragement or feedback to others."

> I felt that my praise was meaningless since I had no direct
> influence over my co-workers. They were my peers, and many
> were my friends. I offered an occasional, "thanks for getting

this done" acknowledgment, but I no longer went out of my way to recognize or praise the performance of my fellow co-workers like I had with my direct reports.

What Alex realized is that when you don't have a leadership title or position, you have to practice leadership through more collegial relationships. As Alex explained: "It is important that my co-workers feel like I appreciate them as individuals and value their contribution to my work and our organization; my work would be impossible without their contribution." For example, Alex was assigned a last-minute marketing video shoot, described by his senior manager as a "dumpster fire" and "impossible." To prepare for it, Peter, the company's field service engineer, had been working 12-hour days for the preceding week and felt exhausted and disgruntled.

Knowing that Peter lived three hours from the project site, Alex decided he would put Peter up in a nice hotel the night before the shoot and take him out to dinner in appreciation of his hard work. As Alex had anticipated, during their dinner together Peter complained about the project's short notice and long hours. Alex listened to his complaints and sympathized with his predicament. Then he said, "I took this moment to express my appreciation for Peter's hard work and made sure he knew that this project would not have been possible without him."

I also let him know that he was the hero of this project and that I had personally asked for him since he had performed at a high level on previous projects. Last, I made sure that Peter knew he was here because I did not possess the skills that he did and that the project was dependent on those skills. I let Peter know that I was confident he had everything under control and that I was confident in his ability to get the job done. I reassured him that I would be on set to help and to let me know if he needed anything to get the job completed.

It was a long day, and the video shoot was a complete success. Afterward, Alex wrote an email to Peter's direct supervisor, the director of his group, and the marketing team to thank Peter for all his hard work and "to give him all the credit." Upon reflecting back on this experience, Alex said, "I realized that putting in the extra effort to personally thank someone, placing them into the spotlight, and encouraging their good work can generate a great deal of good will." Peter's supervisor called to thank him for the email and praise of Peter's performance. Alex also received a message from Peter thanking him and indicating that he could personally request him again for any special projects in the future. "Giving encouragement and thanking someone doesn't require a lot of effort," Alex realized, but the challenge is to actually remember to follow through and do it.

Like so many other leaders with whom we talked, Alex understood the importance of recognizing people for who they are and celebrating what they contribute and accomplish. Time and again, in their Personal-Best Leadership Experiences, people reported working very intensely and for very long hours—and enjoying it. Yet to persist for months at such a pace, people need encouragement, and exemplary leaders are always there to help people find the courage they need to do things that they have never done before.

Leaders give heart to others by recognizing individual contributions and celebrating victories together. These actions signal care and kindness; they show respect, friendliness, and an interest in others. People want to be around those who bestow importance onto others rather than on themselves.[1] Studies show that employees who demonstrate positive affective emotions are likely to experience high degrees of cooperation from their colleagues.[2]

The most effective leaders are those who most frequently engage in the Encourage the Heart leadership practice. Individuals asked their colleagues to complete the LPI–Observer, indicating how often they observed that person engaging in the six leadership behaviors associated with Encourage the Heart. Peers were also asked for an assessment of how effective they found this individual to be as a leader. The statistical analysis showed that effectiveness evaluations increased systematically as peers indicated this individual engaging more and more frequently in these leadership behaviors.

Expect the Best

Believing in people's abilities is essential if you are to make extraordinary things happen; it is an extraordinarily powerful force in propelling performance. Exemplary leaders elicit high performance because they firmly believe in people's abilities to achieve even the most challenging goals. You need to have high expectations, both of yourself and of the people you work with, because these expectations become the frames into which people fit reality. People are much more likely to see what they expect to see, even when their perspectives differ from what actually may be occurring. There's ample research evidence that people act in ways that are consistent with the expectations that other people have of them. If you expect others to fail, they probably will. If you expect them to succeed, they probably will.[3]

It was not unusual to hear from people that they were often anxious, nervous, even scared at the beginning of what would become their Personal-Best Leadership Experience. An important factor that made it possible for them to do something they had never done before was that their own leaders had high expectations for them. Spurred on by these expectations, they developed the self-confidence that gave them the courage and volition to live up to their leaders' expectations. When we asked Don Bennett, the first amputee to climb to the summit of Mt. Rainer, about how he reached the top, he told us about how his teenage daughter stayed by his side during a particularly difficult part of the ascent. She shouted in his ear: "You can do it, Dad. You're the best dad in the world. You can do it, Dad!" Bolstered by that expectation, Don said that there was no way he was going to give up.

Expectations shape how you behave toward others and also influence your own behavior. The high expectations that leaders have of others are based in large part on their expectations of themselves. This is one reason why it is so critical for leaders to Model the Way. Your own record of achievement and dedication, and your daily demonstrations of what and how things need to be accomplished, give credibility to the expectations you have of others.

Exemplary leaders treat people in a way that bolsters their self-confidence, making it possible for them to achieve more than they may have initially believed possible of themselves. Feeling appreciated by others increases a person's sense of self-worth, which in turn, precipitates success at work and home. Research and everyday experience confirm that people with high self-esteem "feel unique, competent, secure, empowered, and connected to the people around them."[4] This is true across all ages, levels of education, and socioeconomic backgrounds. If you have someone in your life who believes in you, and who continually reinforces that belief through his or her interactions with you, you are strongly influenced by that support. You can have the same impact on those you interact with.

Adopt a Winning Attitude   If you want the people you work with to have a winning attitude, you have to believe that they are already winners. It's not that they will be winners someday; they are winners *right now*! If you believe that people are winners, you will treat them that way. Moreover, if you want people to be winners, you have to behave in ways that communicate to them that they are winners. And it's not just about your words. It's also about your tone of voice, posture, gestures, and facial expressions. No yelling, frowning, cajoling, making fun of, or putting them down. Instead, it's about being friendly, positive, supportive, and encouraging. You offer positive reinforcement, share lots of information, listen deeply to people's input, provide sufficient resources to do their jobs, give increasingly challenging assignments, and lend them your support and assistance.

The LPI data shows that the more often co-workers report that their colleague makes it "a point to let people know about his/her confidence in their abilities" the more strongly they agree that they are proud of the organization. As shown in Figure 6, this leadership behavior is also systematically related to this individual's peers' belief that the organization values their work. Rarely engaging in this leadership behavior results in almost no sense of feeling valued. At the other end of the behavioral continuum, more than 70 percent of colleagues and co-workers experience being valued when use of this behavior by the individual is described as very frequent, if not always. Joyce Tan, clinical outsourcing associate for a global pharmaceutical company, gave voice to this finding when she told us: "I've learned from my previous work experience how damaging the lack of positive encouragement is. Being on the receiving end of many demanding requests and not getting any form of recognition, celebration, or encouragement made me question my capabilities at work. I felt burnout and a lack of motivation. However, when I changed jobs, I experienced how life-giving words of encouragement are. You can never be too encouraging."

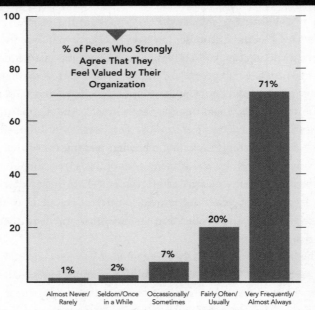

Figure 6 Letting Others Know About Your Confidence in People's Abilities Fuels Their Feelings About Being Valued

% of Peers Who Strongly Agree That They Feel Valued by Their Organization

Frequency with Which Individual Lets Others Know About His/Her Confidence In People's Abilities

It's a virtuous circle: Because you believe in your constituents' abilities, your favorable expectations cause you to be more positive in your actions, and those encouraging behaviors produce better results, reinforcing your belief that people can do it. What's really powerful about this virtuous circle is that as people see that they are capable of extraordinary performance, they develop that expectation of themselves. Another virtuous circle begins.

If the potential exists within someone, you have to find a way to create the conditions that allow the individual to release it. The emerging field of positive organizational psychology provides substantial evidence for this. For example, leaders who create an affirmative orientation in organizations, foster virtuousness among people, and focus on achieving outcomes beyond the norm achieve significantly better results with their staff.[5] There's growing proof that it pays to expect the best and to be positive. Clearly, leaders can find ways, often quite simple, to nurture and bring out the best in those around them.

Positive expectations create positive images in the mind, where positive futures for yourself and others are first constructed. According to researchers, "We see what our imaginative horizon allows us to see."[6] Unless you and others can see yourselves as being successful, it is tough to produce the behavior that leads to success. Positive images make you more effective, relieving symptoms of illness, and enhancing achievement. For example, people who had never participated in bowling were randomly assigned to different groups and instructed in effective techniques. Following these lessons, the bowlers were videotaped practicing. One group of the videotaped bowlers saw only the positive things they did; the other group saw only the negative. Those who saw only their positive moves improved significantly more than any of the other bowlers and were the most interested in continuing with the sport into the future.[7]

Pay Attention to Provide Useful Feedback   Leaders should be out and about. You must make sure that you don't spend all your time in a cubicle, stuck behind a desk, glued to a screen, or fastened to your equipment. Paying attention can't be accomplished very well from a distance—reading reports or hearing information secondhand. You have to be mobile. People want to see you in living color. Proximity is the single best predictor of whether two people will talk to one another, so you have to get close to people if you're going to communicate and know what is going on with them.

You should not be engaged in purposeless wandering. Exemplary leaders are out there for a reason, and one of the most central is to show that you genuinely care because you are *paying attention* to what people are doing as well as to how they are feeling. You have to look past the organizational diagrams, job descriptions, and the formal roles people play and see the person inside. When you are clear about the standards expected and believe that people will perform like winners, then you're going to notice lots of examples of them both doing things right and doing the right things. When you pay attention to what's going on around you, especially with how people are doing and feeling, you develop almost a sixth sense of what people need to know about how they are doing. Because you've been paying attention and been out and about, you are in a credible position to share information that people otherwise might not be privy to.

Another benefit of being out and about is that it increases your own visibility, making you better known to others. You are getting to know other people, and they are also getting to know you. Paying attention and actively appreciating others increases their trust in you. People trust to a much greater extent those they know over those who are strangers to them. If people know you genuinely care about them, they're likely to reciprocate and care about you.

Paying attention provides you with real-time data that allows you to provide those around you with feedback about how they are doing and how they are regarded. Most people wish they received more feedback from their colleagues.[8] As Holly Allen, a records analyst with a global manufacturing company, told us, "Receiving feedback is the most important thing in my growth because without knowing where I am, how can I plan where I need to go? And without a colleague who can point out my mistakes, these can sometimes be overlooked and not corrected."

Take Holly's sentiments to heart and consider what happens to people's self-confidence without feedback. In one study, researchers told people that their efforts would be compared with how well hundreds of others had done on the same task. They subsequently received praise, criticism, or no feedback on their performance. Those who heard nothing about how well they did suffered as great a blow to their self-confidence as those criticized. Only those who received positive feedback improved their performance.[9] Saying nothing about a person's performance doesn't help anyone—not the performer, not the leader, not the organization. People want to know how they are doing, and they actually would prefer to hear bad news rather than no news at all. They prefer to know how they are doing, and no news has the same negative impact as bad news. Which is precisely what Hilary Hall, a global strategy lead for a worldwide provider of food, agriculture, financial, and industrial services, told us was the key lesson from her Personal-Best Leadership Experience: "It can be somewhat of a painful and embarrassing experience," she said, "to admit that there are parts of us that are unflattering, but it is a necessary component of self-reflection and growth."

However, we've found in our research that seeking feedback is not that easy for people to do, regardless of their hierarchical position. On the LPI, the leadership behavior that individual contributors and managers alike consistently report engaging in least frequently is "asks for feedback on how my actions affect other people's performance." You can't learn very much if you're unwilling to find out more about how your actions are affecting the behavior and performance of those around you.

Being interested in information about how you are doing is characteristic of the best learners, and it's something all people, and especially leaders, need to cultivate. "Focusing on asking for feedback and giving people a safe space and opportunity to provide feedback," was an area for growth that Amy Tomlinson identified as she took on responsibility for business development at a startup company working to build clean power infrastructure throughout North America. As one example of how she implemented this leadership behavior at work, Amy told us, "I intentionally asked my new co-workers and my boss the following questions: 'How do you think that meeting went? Was the meeting what you were hoping for? Was there anything I could have provided or done better for you during the meeting?'" This was in contrast to questions she had previously asked to invite feedback, framing them as specific to her and her performance, such as "How did I do?" or "What could I have done better?" Amy noticed that posing her questions more about the process than about herself not only produced more useful feedback, but it also resulted in "many side-bar 'deeper' conversations being initiated, co-workers fessing up about areas that were challenging them, healthy dialogues around possible solutions, and where assistance or encouragement would be welcomed." You have an opportunity, as Amy's experience demonstrates, to provide the necessary encouragement for the people you are working with to make improvements to their current situations.

Develop Friendships Managerial myth says leaders shouldn't get too close to their colleagues and leaders can't be friends with people at work. Well, set this myth aside. Over a five-year period, researchers observed groups of friends and groups of acquaintances (people who knew each other only slightly) performing motor-skill and decision-making tasks. The results were unequivocal. The groups composed of friends completed, on average, more than three times as many projects as the groups consisting merely of acquaintances. Regarding decision-making assignments, groups of friends were over 20 percent more effective than groups of acquaintances were.[10]

Researchers have also found that having friends at work is good for your health, as well as for productivity. Those who report that they have a "best friend at work" are significantly more engaged, get more done in less time, have a safer workplace with fewer accidents, share ideas, feel informed, are innovative, and indicate having more fun on the job.[11] And there are plenty of prospects for strengthening these relationships, because fewer than one in five people indicate that they work for organizations that provide opportunities to develop friendships in their workplace.[12]

There is an important caveat, however. You and your friends have to be firmly committed to the group's goals. If not, then groups of friends may not do better. This is precisely why it is necessary for you to be clear about standards and create a foundation of shared vision and values. When it comes to performance, commitment to standards and good interpersonal relations go together.

People are more willing to follow someone they like and trust. To become fully trusted, as we previously noted, you have to ante up first by being open yourself—open to others, and open *with* others. Just as an open door is a physical demonstration of a willingness to let others in, an open heart is an emotional one. This means letting others know more about you, what you care about, why you make the choices you do, and so forth. We don't mean tabloid-style disclosures. We mean talking about your aspirations, your family and friends, your interests and your pursuits—the same things you'd like to know about other people.

When you open up, you make yourself vulnerable—and this vulnerability is what makes you more human and more trustworthy to others. If neither person in a relationship takes the risk of trusting, at least a little, the relationship remains stalled at the level of caution and suspicion, and there's no way to build a caring connection. If leaders want the higher levels of performance that come with trust and collaboration, then they must demonstrate their trust *in* others before asking for trust *from* others.

Disclosing information can be risky. You can't be sure that other people will appreciate your candor, empathize with your experiences, agree with your aspirations, buy into your plans, or interpret your words and actions in the way you intend. But in demonstrating the willingness to take such risks, you encourage others to take a similar risk and thereby take the first necessary steps to find common ground for building mutual trust.

Researchers have found that in addition to developing friendships at work, being positive around your co-workers pays dividends.[13] People who authentically display positive emotions feel better at work, reporting lower levels of fatigue and emotional exhaustion. They indicate they are more productive because of the help they receive from their colleagues—both personal (someone listens to my problems and concerns) and task-related (someone offers assistance when demands get out of hand). Consequently, they also strongly feel that they can trust their co-workers.

Personalize Recognition It seems obvious but in order to personalize recognition you have to know the people you are working with, and this begins simply with knowing their names. It's difficult to imagine that you can have a relationship with another person when you don't even know his or her name, or some of the key things about them, like whether they have a spouse/partner, a family, interests outside of work, and so on. Get to know the people you are working with, because when you know people, then you can recognize them in a way that they personally value, because it's relevant to what they care about. Jennifer Lee echoed this perspective in her Personal-Best Leadership Experience: "I needed to understand what drove each individual to do better and how each liked being recognized and rewarded. For some it was gift cards, for others meals, and so on. There was no one size that fit all." What's required is getting to know your colleagues so you can recognize them in a way that they personally value.

When we've asked people to tell us about their *most meaningful recognitions,* they consistently reported that they are "personal." They say that it felt special. "A sincere word of thanks from the right person at the right time," other researchers have noted, "can mean more to an employee than a raise, a formal award, or a whole wall of certificates and plaques."[14] And yet a familiar complaint about recognition is that it's too often highly predictable and impersonal. A one-size-fits-all approach to recognition feels disingenuous, forced, and thoughtless. It's like how birthday celebrations are done at restaurants. The staff sings to someone, and people at other tables start singing, even though they don't know the person. No matter how well intended, over time these routines can increase cynicism and actually damage credibility.

You have to do more than provide drive-by praise, simply walking around your organization or community saying, "Thank you, whoever you are, for whatever you are doing." It is essential to pay attention to the likes and dislikes of each person you work with. To make recognition meaningful, you have to tailor it to their needs, values, and aspirations. By personalizing recognition, you send the message that you took the time to notice an achievement, sought out the responsible individual, and delivered the appreciation in a timely manner.

As a coach for the girl's developmental team associated with a Major League Soccer club, Stephanie Sorg recognized that many of her actions were "unintentionally bland and repetitive, and as a result, my players failed to feel appreciated or fully motivated." She told us, "I needed to make it a priority to stoke the individual fires in each person in order to foster a healthy atmosphere that encouraged improvement." Stephanie started paying more attention to the needs of the players and less time on the game fundamentals, dedicating more time toward recognizing their efforts and meeting with the players individually to express her satisfaction with their efforts. She had to get close enough to them so that she could comment on specific things they were doing, as well as genuinely express her commitment to and interest in them.

As Stephanie's experience illustrates, if you're going to personalize recognition and make it feel genuinely special, you'll have to look past the organization charts and roles people play and see the person inside. You need to get to know how your co-workers feel, and what they think. You can do it one-on-one or in group settings, but the key message is to pay attention to them individually *and* as team. Let them know you are noticing their interests, their habits, their strengths, and their needs. Armed with this information you will be better able to build the connections between people and ensure that the people you are working with identify as part of the team and community.

One way to build those connections is what Kevin Jiang, senior product engineer for a computer game company, reported in his Personal-Best Leadership Experience. "I always sent out appreciative emails to team members for achieving each milestone," he said. "I pointed out each individual's contributions during project meetings and bolded their names in meeting minutes. I ensured that their managers were in the same email loop, so that upper-level management could know that those people did a great job." Kevin asked people to explain what and why they did what they did, and by showing an interest in the story behind the accomplishment he honored both the results as well as the person who achieved them.[15] Acknowledging people's accomplishments makes them feel valued and trusted, reinforces the progress being made, and inspires that individual, and others, to even greater effort and levels of performance.

People are more willing to follow someone they feel knows who they are and what they need. Feeling a connection with others motivates people to work harder for the simple reason that people don't like to disappoint or let down individuals they consider friends. People also stick around longer in organizations and groups when they feel they have colleagues who know them and have their best interests at heart.

Personalized recognition comes down to being *thoughtful*. You need to be authentic and sincerely care about that person. Take those observations you've made about an individual and ask: "What would really make this special and unique for her? What could I do to make this a memorable experience so that he always remembers how important his contributions are?"

Use a Creative Mix of Recognitions   Personalization also enables you to be more creative in your approach to recognition. Jeremy Moser was captain of his collegiate champion tennis team when he learned an important lesson from his Personal-Best Leadership Experience: "Not every person works the same or is triggered by the same incentive, which means you have to get to know every single person on your team and find out what that particular person desires and how to use that to motivate them."

Don't make the mistake of assuming that people respond only to formal or monetary rewards. People respond to all kinds of informal acknowledgments. Verbal recognition of performance in front of one's peers and visible reminders, such as certificates, plaques, trophies, and mementos, are also powerful commemorations of achievements. Karina Chamorro received a staff award at a grand ceremony, and she told us that what meant the most to her "was reading the nominations written by my manager and peers. It was having my work seen and appreciated by my peers that propelled me to a new level of commitment." Generally, individual displays of gratitude carry as much, if not more, weight than formal rewards (a promotion, bonus, etc.).

There are numerous ways you can show your appreciation that are within your scope of influence and ability. For example, you can send a handwritten note (even better than an email, like, or tweet), make a comment in a meeting about someone's good work or achievement, or just stop by the person's workspace to let him or her know that you are aware of the great work he or she is doing. Taking these ideas to heart, Emily Leiter, medical device sales analyst, told us about how she wanted to express her appreciation to one of the company's information technology professionals, who had worked a few weekends to help her complete a project. Instead of giving him her usual "thank-you" of a Starbucks' gift card, she remembered that he wasn't much of a coffee drinker, and that he had a large family, so she decided to buy him a gift card to The Cheesecake Factory so that he could take his whole family out to dinner and spend time with them to make up for not seeing them much while he was working weekends. Emily was not only personalizing her recognition but also "hoping that by working hard to creatively show my appreciation, people would see that I really value them as people."

Spontaneous and unexpected rewards, people have told us, are typically more meaningful than the expected formal rewards. And to make it the most effective, be sure that your recognition is highly specific and given in close proximity to the appropriate behavior. Being too general or too late diminishes the positive power of the gesture. As Rachelle Mata Castaneda described in her Personal-Best Leadership Experience, championing the sales efforts of the city's convention and visitors bureau, "We were very mindful of accomplishments along the way. We had potlucks, meals out together, recognitions at team meetings, and so on. We were generous with compliments, and as a result we felt good about ourselves, and when you feel good you are more productive."

Often, it's the simple, personal gestures that are the most powerful rewards. Personal congratulations rank at the top of the most powerful non-financial motivators identified by employees.[16] There are few, if any, more basic needs than being noticed, recognized, and appreciated for your efforts. Institutions with the greatest volume of appreciation tend to be the most innovative and vibrant organizations. Clearly, not enough people make sufficient use of that powerful but inexpensive two-word reward, "thank you."

It is always worth the time to recognize someone's hard work and contributions. All too often, people forget to extend a hand, offer a smile, or express a simple thank you. Studies clearly reveal that those who feel appreciated for their work are more productive and stick around the workplace longer. People feel frustrated, and seldom work to their capacity, when their efforts and achievements are taken for granted. Sometimes they will overlook this, knowing that others might be under the pressure of deadlines, and the mandate to deliver on time overtakes expressing gratitude. However, it's critical that you stick around for that extra moment to extend a simple pat on the back, a handshake, a smile, and a "Thank you for your hard work." Doing so not only increases productivity, but it can actually save lives, as shown in one study involving bus drivers, where receiving appreciation resulted in fewer accidents and avoidable incidents on the roads.[17]

The wonderful thing about expressing appreciation and providing recognition is that these aren't hard to do, and you don't need to be seated on a hierarchical perch to dispense them. They cost you next to nothing, and yet pay daily dividends. You can't ask for a better investment than that. Researchers have found that people who practice gratitude, compared to those who do not, are healthier, more optimistic, more positive, and better able to cope with stress. They are also more alert, more energized, more resilient, more willing to offer support to others, more generous, and more likely to make progress toward important goals.[18]

Create a Spirit of Community

Human beings are social animals—hardwired to connect with others.[19] People are meant to do things together, to form communities, and in this way demonstrate a common bond. When social connections are strong and numerous, there's more trust, reciprocity, information flow, collective action, and happiness—and, by the way, greater prosperity.[20] Teams perform better when their members believe that their colleagues respect and appreciate them.[21] Online retailer Warby Parker routinely holds "lunch roulette," where employees from different departments are randomly selected to enjoy lunch on the company's nickel in an effort to promote cross-functional connections and a sense of community.[22]

In order to provide meaningful recognition, it is essential for leaders to create a spirit of community. In days past, it used to be said that seven was the maximum number of people who could report up the chain of command. These days, when asked that question, we say that it depends on how many people you can remember—their names, what they do, where they are from, something about their personal relationships, their aspirations, and so on. The same may be said for individual contributors and those dealing with lateral and horizontal relationships. After all, leadership, as we've maintained, is all about relationships. Increased social contact, whether in-person or virtual, not only improves people's moods but boosts productivity as well. In a study of 25,000 call center agents, they were divided into two groups—one who took staggered breaks alone and the other who took breaks with their co-workers. Those who had 15 minutes to socialize and chat with colleagues had a 20 percent increase in performance over their peers who did not.[23]

In a similar way, you don't need to be in any particular position or to be someone's supervisor in order to contribute to creating a community spirit. Andy Ramans, senior manufacturing engineer with a firm providing minimally invasive surgical equipment, wondered whether people would value having one of their colleagues say, "Thank you" or "Good job." At first he thought these words would be wasted, but then he reflected about how he felt when his colleagues thanked or praised him. "That's when I realized the power of recognizing and appreciating others," he said. Friends and friendships thrive when people feel that they are not being taken for granted. When their contributions are acknowledged, even by their colleagues and their peers around them, they know that they are making a difference and feel connected not only to some shared outcome but to one another.

All over the world, in every country, in every culture, and in every organization and community, people stop working on certain days during the year and take the time to celebrate. Impromptu ceremonies are often convened to rejoice in the publication of a new marketing effort, the launch of a new service, the opening of a new facility or art installation, receipt of some civic or professional award, and the like. Banquets are organized to acknowledge individuals and groups who've accomplished the extraordinary. Colleagues get together with one another at the conclusion of working on an exhausting task force and give each other high-fives for a job well done. Even in tragic times, people come together in remembrance and song to honor those before them and to reaffirm their common humanity.

Why do people take time away from work to gather together, tell stories, and raise their spirits? Sure, everyone needs a break from the pace and intensity of their jobs, but celebrating is not a frivolous excuse to goof off. Celebrations are among the most significant ways people have to proclaim their respect and gratitude, renew their sense of community, and remind themselves of their shared values and traditions. Celebrations serve as important a purpose in the long-term health of organizations and communities as does the performance of daily tasks.

What leaders know from practice is confirmed in our research. Performance improves when they bring people together to rejoice in their achievements and to reinforce their shared principles. Individual recognition increases the recipient's sense of worth, and it improves performance. Public celebrations have this effect *and more*. Every time you can get your group together is a chance to renew commitment. Exemplary leaders seldom let pass any opportunity to make sure that everyone knows why they're all there and how they're going to act in service of that purpose. Whether the occasion is to honor an individual, group, or organizational achievement, celebrations offer leaders the perfect opening to explicitly communicate and reinforce the actions and behaviors that are important in realizing shared values and shared goals.

Provide Social Support Supportive relationships at work—relationships characterized by a genuine belief in and advocacy for the interests of others—are critically important to maintaining personal and organizational vitality. Researchers have found that in top-performing teams, people give each other 5.6 positive comments for every criticism. This ratio falls down to about two positive comments for every negative one in medium-performing teams, and it falls even more dramatically for the poorest-performing teams. In those teams, members give nearly three times the number of negative comments for every positive one![24]

Performance improves when leaders provide social support by publicly honoring those who have excelled and been an example to others. It also goes up when you can demonstrate that "we are all in this together," and when you make the work environment a place where people want to be, stay, and work hard. It was a terrible blow for Renee Calvert and her tight-knit, online community when the show they were fans of faced potential cancellation because accusations of misconduct by the show's creator surfaced. She wanted to infuse the community with positivity and unity and took it upon herself to remind everyone that the show they loved involved more people—the writers, voice actors, animators, and others— who were not at fault. To cheer up the fan community, Renee invited members to join an online gift exchange. Handcrafted gifts related to the show would be contributed and received by all who joined. The response was overwhelming. People posted and praised photos of others' work. They started talking more about their values than the situation with the creator. Renee helped them realize they could focus on supporting each other and the values that drew them together in the first place. An extensive ten-year study backs up Renee's experience in revealing that social support networks are essential for sustaining the motivation to serve. Service-performance shortfalls in organizations are highly correlated with the absence of social support and teamwork.[25] Co-workers who support each other and achieve together can be an antidote to service burnout. Working with others should be rejuvenating, inspirational, and even fun.

Enduring human connections produce spectacular results when leaders and constituents alike are personally involved with the task and with their colleagues. When people feel a strong sense of affiliation and attachment to the people with whom they are working, they're much more likely to experience greater personal well-being, to feel more committed to the organization, and to perform at higher levels. When people feel distant and detached, they're unlikely to get much of anything significant done at all. Longitudinal studies, in the United States and Europe, have found that people who make use of social support have higher incomes compared to those people who don't tap into the power of a social network. This was true both two and nine years after the study's baseline period.[26] Lacking social support, individuals regularly ignored cooperative opportunities, distrusting other people and their motives. Studies involving more than three million people around the world show that social isolation is worse for people's health than obesity, smoking, and alcoholism.[27]

Being alone makes people miserable. Celebrations remind people that they're not alone in their efforts and that they both need and can count on one another to make things happen and achieve success. These reminders build the courage to continue in times of turmoil and stress. They reinforce the fact that it takes a group of people working together with a common purpose, in an atmosphere of trust and collaboration, to achieve the extraordinary.

The case for social support is further boosted by the fact that information exchange is more likely to be facilitated, whether in formal or informal interactions, when people like one another. Even in the age of social media, people are just more likely to share things when they're in a gathering with other people, even a virtual one, than when they're sitting alone at their workstations or on their mobiles. When celebrations cut across functional and hierarchical boundaries, people get a chance to exchange ideas with, and be stimulated by, people outside their own areas.

By making achievements public, leaders build a culture in which people know that their actions and decisions are not being taken for granted. They see that their contributions are recognized, appreciated, and valued, and are more likely to repeat such actions again in the future. Technical project manager Andrea Berardo recalled one of his "nicest memories of working" with a European-based power company was an informal, privately funded party to celebrate the successful past of their department in view of some upcoming major organizational changes. It was important, he said, to make sure that everyone received positive feedback and words of encouragement: "Public celebrations, in my experience, are crucial to the self-esteem of the employees, and they are essential in building that sense of community that allows people to see themselves as part of one team." Andrea pointed out another benefit for leaders and their co-workers: "Public events are perfect occasions to reiterate the shared values and common goals."

Celebrate and Have Some Fun   Shifts in the psychological contract between employers and employees, workforce demographics, and changes in the work itself are necessitating that people experience their organizations as a place that they can do more than just work, that they can have fun.[28] A fun work environment "intentionally encourages, initiates, and supports a variety of enjoyable and pleasurable activities that positively impact the attitude and productivity of individuals and groups."[29] Researchers have shown that such workplaces contribute positively to affective, cognitive, and behavioral functioning of employees.[30]

Celebrations should be fun; and fun isn't a luxury at work. Every Personal-Best Leadership Experience was a combination of hard work and fun. In fact, most people agreed that without the enjoyment and the pleasure they experienced interacting with others on the team, they would have been unable to sustain the level of intensity and hard work required to achieve their personal best. People just feel better about the work they're doing when they enjoy the people they're working with.[31]

Having fun sustains productivity, creating what researchers refer to as "subjective well-being." Moreover, it's not all about parties, games, festivities, and laughter. Wayne Tam, a certified financial planner, described one of his colleagues as someone who really had fun dissecting complex computer code or translating business processes into functional specifications. Wayne said that these tasks could be quite difficult, but this person was always positive and made him and others feel that they could all meet such challenges with the same attitude. He also showed them how to have fun with this type of work. Wayne went on to say, "I learned that though you get paid to do a job, it's better to be able to enjoy what you do and have fun."

Research demonstrates that having fun enhances people's problem-solving skills. They are more creative and productive, which fosters lower turnover, higher morale, and a stronger bottom line. For example, the Great Place to Work Institute annually asks tens of thousands of employees to rate their experience of workplace factors, including, "This is a fun place to work." On Fortune's 100 Best Companies to Work For list, which the Great Place to Work Institute produces, employees in the best organizations responded overwhelmingly—an average of 81 percent—that they are working in a "fun" environment.[32] According to Robert Provine, a neuroscientist at the University of Maryland and author of *Laughter: A Scientific Investigation*, "laughter is not primarily about humor, but about social relationships. In fact, the health benefits of laughter may result from the social support it stimulates."[33]

Often it seems like celebrating in the workplace is a managerial prerogative, but who says that has to be the case? There are no limits to the informal ways that you and your colleagues can celebrate with one another, from personal achievements to organizational milestones. When you openly demonstrate the joy and passion you have for the work and service you and your colleagues are providing, it is contagious. Work in today's organizations is often very demanding, and to sustain their commitment people need to have a sense of personal well-being while on the job. Everyone benefits when people show enthusiasm and excitement about the work performed. You spend so many hours of your life at work, you should be enjoying it. What are some ways you can sneak in a little lightheartedness when things are really tense? As so many told us in their Personal-Best Leadership Experiences: "If the team is enjoying the work they are doing, and feeling recognized for their hard work, they are likely to go the extra mile."

Celebrations should be fun, but that shouldn't be their primary purpose. They're ceremonies and rituals that create meaning. Any celebration must be an honest expression of commitment to fundamental values and appreciation for the hard work and dedication of the people who have lived the values. Elaborate productions that lack sincerity are more entertainment than encouragement. Authenticity makes celebrations purposeful and fun. At these occasions, it's vitally important to be clear about the behaviors you want to reinforce. You should be fully aware that people are going to leave the event remembering and repeating what you say about what is being recognized. Celebrations, the data shows, significantly affect how people feel about their organization and their leader.

Be Personally Involved   Wherever you find a culture built around shared values, you'll also find endless examples of leaders who personally live those values. You make values tangible by putting them into action. There are countless ways to live your values in all kinds of organizations. For example, in an academic setting, the residential adviser demonstrates it by choosing the less desirable suite because it's closest to the central hub of the building. In the workplace, it's the IT specialist who comes in on the weekend to protect the network from a potential cyber attack, or a master scheduler for the solar roofing company who returns calls from her home in the evening when she can't connect with customers during the day. In the home, it's the parents who give their own bedroom to their kids so that they have enough space for all their toys and stuffed animals to be close by. It's the same for people in social service organizations who reschedule vacations in order to help staff their booth at the community's annual street fair, or the people who finish up their work assignments after dinner so that they can take afternoons off to coach youth sports, or the teachers who volunteer to provide childcare so that parents can attend PTA meetings. They are all personally demonstrating that the shared values matter.

It's the same with the leadership practice of Encourage the Heart, whether through individual recognition or group celebration, you have to be personally involved. The LPI data shows that leadership effective-ness assessments by peers are directly related with how often they observe that colleague getting "personally involved in recognizing people and cel-ebrating accomplishments." The best way to show people that you genu-inely care and that you appreciate their efforts is to be with them. Authenticity goes up when you become personally involved. You send a positive signal that you want others to be successful when you directly and visibly show others that you care and cheer them along. Moreover, you're more likely to see others take these same actions if you do them.

Often being personally involved is simply just making sure that you take the time and effort to "hang out" with your colleagues. The benefits were readily apparent to Kim-Ha Ho, finance professional, when she switched up her lunch routine from eating at her desk to regularly having meals and taking breaks in the staff room. Some people might have thought that lunching at her desk meant she didn't care to spend time with them, but that was never her intention. Kim said that when she started eating in the staff room it didn't take long to be included in lively conversations about work and non-work-related issues. Her presence and participation gave witness to her espoused values of openness, kind-ness, family, respect, and teamwork. This change in routine also gave her colleagues the opportunity to ask her about what she's doing, make suggestions, and fill her in on "things" that Kim had been missing while cooped up in her office.

Another benefit of becoming personally involved in showing that you care is that it provides you with an opportunity to find and create stories that put a human face on values. Stories help form a personal bond between you and your listeners by triggering thoughts of shared experiences, background, and struggles.[34] First-person examples are more powerful and memorable than third-party examples. It's that striking difference between "I saw it for myself" and "Someone told me about it." You should constantly be on the lookout for opportunities to "catch people doing things right," and this isn't done very well by staying behind a desk, counter, computer screen, or steering wheel.

You need to see and know firsthand what's being done right, not only so that you can let individuals and teams know to "keep up the good work," but also so that you can tell others about their actions that make a difference. As a result, you can share up-close-and-personal accounts of what it actually means in a real-time context to put shared values into practice. You make values more than pronouncements; you make them come alive. You create role models within your organization or community that everyone can relate to.

Telling stories about how people demonstrate their commitment to values is another way to show your personal involvement, and it is one of the quickest and most effective ways to communicate how people are supposed to act and make decisions.[35] Storytelling has been shown to accomplish the objectives of teaching, mobilizing, and motivating better than bullet points in a slide presentation or tweets on a mobile device. Listening to and understanding the stories that you tell inform people more about the values and actions you most pay attention to than company policy declarations or the employee manual. Stories communicate what really goes on within the organization. Well-told stories reach inside people and pull them along. They simulate the actual experience of being there and give people an emotionally compelling way of learning what is really important about the experience. Reinforcing them through celebrations deepens the connections.

It's the human connection that ensures more commitment and more support. While Lisa Millora holds the title of senior assistant provost at a small-sized college, none of the faculty reports to her. Even so, she sees to it that they know that what they do has an impact by finding ways to recognize them across the campus. Creating a spirit of community to celebrate victories, and hosting celebrations from time to time, has characterized her entire career. With student groups, she takes the time to gather them together and distribute certificates or small tokens of appreciation. According to Lisa, none of these have to be a grand event. She says it's "really just a spirit of gathering." Finding a way to say thank-you—and genuinely meaning it—is a very concrete method of showing respect and enhancing personal credibility, especially when you have no organizational requirement to do so.

We started the discussion of The Five Practices of Exemplary Leadership with Model the Way, and here we are again. If you want others to believe in something and behave according to those beliefs, you have to be personally involved and set the example. You have to practice what you preach. If you want people to stay true to shared values, you have to stay true to them as well. If you want to build and maintain a culture of excellence and distinction, then you have to recognize, reward, reinforce, and celebrate exceptional efforts and successes. You have to be personally involved in celebrating the actions that contribute to and sustain the culture. And, if you want people to have the courage to continue the quest in the face of great adversity, you have to encourage them yourself.

Take Action to Encourage the Heart

Leaders expect to do their best, and they expect the best of others. When leaders provide a clear sense of direction and feedback along the way, they help people focus on what needs to be done. By paying attention, offering encouragement, personalizing appreciation, and maintaining a positive outlook, leaders stimulate, rekindle, and concentrate people's energies and drive. Encouragement is more personal and positive than other forms of feedback, and it strengthens trust within relationships.

You need to recognize individual contributions to vision and values and be creative in demonstrating appreciation. Celebrating values and victories together reinforces the fact that extraordinary performance is the result of many people's efforts. By celebrating people's accomplishments visibly, and in group settings, you nourish and sustain a team spirit. Telling stories about individuals who have made exceptional efforts and achieved phenomenal successes provides role models for others to emulate. Social interaction increases people's commitments to the standards of the group and has a profound effect on people's well-being. By becoming personally involved in recognition and celebrations, you set the example and create a supportive culture of community.

Here are two recommended actions that you should take to continuously strengthen your competence in the leadership practice of Encourage the Heart:

Recognize Contributions. Part of providing meaningful recognition is working to understand what's important to the people you're praising. When you know what people feel confident, self-conscious, enthused, and discouraged about, you know better *how* to show your appreciation of them and what they do in ways that will personally energize them. Learn about how your words and actions can make the biggest difference with each of your colleagues and use that understanding to help them when and where they need it most. As you get to know the people you work with better, you will likely discover non-work-related activities and interests that are also ripe for recognition. Remember that it is also important to acknowledge progress and what's being learned, and not just the final outcome.

Celebrate the Values and Victories. Consider what you can do to ensure that the people you work with know that you and their colleagues are appreciative of how they demonstrate shared values and standards in their work. Create a moment to speak out about the team's achievement or send out an email announcement and copy in the appropriate hierarchical manager. It's great when these can feel spontaneous and unexpected, and it also works to schedule a time to celebrate with one another. In either case, make sure that you say something that makes clear the reason for the recognition—that is, what was done that deserves to be acknowledged—and how it ties back to shared values and aspirations. When you publicly recognize and celebrate exemplary behavior, it has an impact on everyone.

In the final chapter is a reminder that leadership development is fundamentally the development of one's self and a set of strategies and activities you can take to learn how to be the best leader you can be.

CHAPTER 7

Leadership Development Is Self-Development

CONGRATULATIONS ON REACHING this milestone—consider finishing this book a small win in your journey to become the best leader you can be. Let's take a brief look back at the territory you've covered.

The central theme has been that *leadership is everyone's business* as conveyed through the experiences and data about people who have no hierarchical positions, organizational authority, or direct reports, yet were able to make extraordinary things happen. These individuals come from different generations and diverse walks of life and nationalities. They represent a wide variety of organizations, small and large, public and private, government and NGOs, high-tech and low-tech, schools and professional services, and come from urban, suburban, and rural communities. They are employees in workplaces where they are often referred to as individual contributors, analysts, specialists, or associates, and they are also community volunteers, social activists, and family members.

Chances are you haven't previously heard of any of the people mentioned in this book. They're not public figures or famous megastars. They are people who could live next door to you, work in the next cubicle over, or be on that next Zoom call. In short, they are people just like you.

The focus has been on everyday leaders because leadership is not about title or status. It's not about position power or authority. It's not about celebrity or monetary status. It's not about personality, genetics, or the family and circumstance you were born into. It's definitely not about having any super powers or being a hero.

The key message is that you don't have to look up for leadership, and you don't have to look out for leadership. You only have to look inward. *You* have the potential to lead others to places they have never been. Leadership is fundamentally about your relationships, your credibility, and what you *do*. Leadership has everything to do about how you behave.

Leadership Matters

Throughout this book you've seen empirical evidence showing that frequent use of The Five Practices has a positive impact on engagement and on team and organizational performance. Take a moment to test these findings against your own personal experiences with the supervisors, managers, bosses, and leaders you have worked with.

Begin by thinking about the *worst leader* you have ever worked with. Next, write down a number at the end of this sentence representing the percentage, from one to 100, of your talents (skills and abilities plus time and energy) that this worst leader utilized: _____.

Now think about the *best* leader you've ever worked with. Write down a number at the end of this sentence representing the percentage of your talents that your best leader utilized: _____.

We asked this same question of thousands of people from around the globe, and you can see the results in Figure 7. Compare your responses to those we've surveyed. We hypothesize that there's a significant difference between the percentages you gave to your worst and best leaders, right? Remember, it is still you in both cases. The only thing that changed was the behavior of your supervisor.

Figure 7 The Best Leaders Bring Out Three Times the Talents of People, Compared with the Worst Leaders

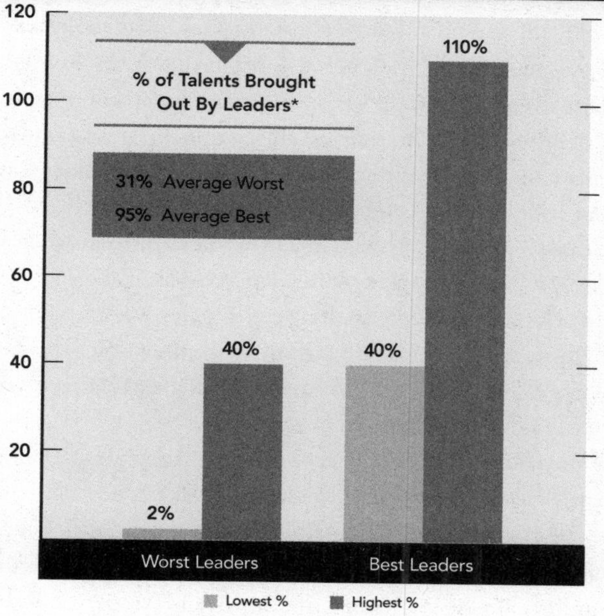

% of Talents Brought
Out By Leaders*

31% Average Worst
95% Average Best

110%

120

100

80

60

40%   40%

40

20

2%

Worst Leaders   Best Leaders

Lowest %   Highest %

**The Range of Their Talents People Report Being
Utilized by Their Worst and Best Leaders**

*Totals more than 100% because people said the best leaders enabled them
to do more than they thought they were capable of

As you can see, when people think about their experience with their *worst* leaders, the percentage of talent utilized typically ranges between 2 percent and 40 percent, with an average of 31 percent. In other words, people report that they expended less than a third of their available skills and abilities working with their worst leaders. Many continued to work hard, but few put all that they were capable of delivering into their efforts. A few responded that they put in nearly 80 percent or more, but that was simply because they not only had to do their own jobs, but also the work of their worst leader!

This dismal situation is in sharp contrast to what people report when they think about their experiences working with their best leaders. Even for those who report that these leaders bring out only about 40 percent of their talent—and usually these are people who explain that they do their best work, irrespective of who their supervisor/manager/leader is—it should be noted that this *bottom* was the *top* of the range for the *worst* leaders. Not infrequently, many people indicate that their best leaders actually got more than 100 percent of their talent! It might seem mathematically impossible to get more than 100 percent of an individual's talent, yet when challenged on this point, these respondents uniformly shake their heads and say, "No, that leader really did get me to do more than I thought I was capable of doing or that it seemed was even possible to do." The *average* percentage of talent utilized when working with their best leaders is a whopping 95 percent.

The performance difference between people's worst and best leaders is huge. The best leaders bring out more than three times the amount of talent, energy, and motivation from their people compared with their counterparts at the other end of the spectrum.

This data, and other evidence presented throughout this book, confirms that *leadership makes a difference*. That difference can be negative or it can be positive, but it certainly does matter. Leadership has an impact on people's commitment, their willingness to put forth discretionary effort, to take personal initiative and responsibility, and to perform beyond the ordinary. Inept leaders have a dampening effect on these behaviors, and exemplary leaders have just the opposite effect.

The difference that the exemplary leaders can have is evident in this example that Verónica Guerrero related in one of our classes. We asked participants to share a story about a leader they admired and whose direction they would willingly follow. She chose her father, José Luis Guerrero. Verónica spoke about her father's leadership in the Unión Nacional Sinarquista (UNS) back in the early 1940s. (UNS later became part of another political party—Partido Demócrata Mexicano [PDM], or Mexican Democratic Party.) She related in detail what her father did and then summed up his influence with this recollection from José Luis: "I think the work that I did back then helped me extend myself and others to levels that I didn't know I could reach. . . . If you feel strongly about anything, and it's something that will ultimately benefit your community and your country, don't hold back. Fear of failing or fear of what might happen doesn't help anyone. . . . Don't let anyone or anything push you back."

Verónica closed the description of her father (who was then dying of pancreatic cancer) with this observation: "As I heard his story and I saw a sick, tired, and weak man, I couldn't help thinking that our strength as humans and as leaders has nothing to do with what we look like. Rather, it has everything to do with what we feel, what we think of ourselves. . . . Leadership is applicable to all facets of life."

That's precisely the point. If you are to learn to be a better leader, you must first believe that you are capable of leadership and that you can be a positive force in the world.

Leadership Can Be Learned

You want to become the best leader you can be or otherwise you would not be reading this book! Becoming the best leader is a moral imperative; you owe it to the people for whom you are a role model, for the people you work with, for the people your products serve, and for the success of the endeavors you are pursuing.

Still, the question often arises as to whether or not everyone is capable of exercising leadership, engaging in the leadership behaviors associated with The Five Practices. The data from the *Leadership Practices Inventory* provides remarkably consistent proof.[1] This 360-degree assessment provides information on how often individuals are currently engaging in the leadership behaviors and actions that are associated with people being at their personal best as leaders. The LPI is comprised of 30 leadership behaviors. Each behavior is assessed on a 10-point frequency scale from "1," indicating that this individual "almost never" engages in that specific behavior to "10," indicating that he or she "almost always" engages in the behavior described. The LPI provides a 360-degree look— from the leader's self-perspective, as well as the vantage point of their managers, colleagues, direct reports, and others—at the extent to which the actions identified as essential leadership behaviors are being used.

In over 35 years of collecting data on leadership behaviors practically *no one* who completed the LPI has scored a "zero" across all five leadership practices. To do so would mean that the individual (or their manager, colleagues, and/or direct reports) reported that they "almost never" engaged in any of the 30 leadership behaviors. Since 2004, with over 3.52 million respondents, the total number of people reporting a "zero" is 581, for a percentage of .0165. Do the math, and you will find that in an organization with 100 employees, the probability of finding an individual with "zero" leadership behaviors is ZERO. And make that a 1,000-person organization and the probability is still zero, and even in a 10,000-person enterprise, the probability remains less than two people. And, if you only included in these calculations respondents who were not in management positions, the percentage of zeros (I almost never engaged in any of these 30 leadership behaviors) is even more unlikely (0.0074). The percentage of peers who assess one of their colleagues to never engage in any of these 30 leadership behaviors is even more remote (0.0054).

The empirical findings and mathematical results support the assertion that everyone is capable of engaging in leadership behaviors. In fact, almost everyone is exhibiting *some* (*more than "almost never"*) leadership behaviors already. The chances of finding someone in your most immediate group who cannot exercise leadership is zero. At the same time, it would be an exaggeration to claim that because 99.9835 percent of people are already demonstrating some leadership behaviors that everyone *will* become an exemplary leader. Not every person in a family, organization, community, or nation will want to make the commitment or devote the energy and effort to become exemplary.

We are certain, however, that no matter your current level of skill and ability, you can more frequently exercise leadership than you do now. The reason for investing the time and energy to become a better leader is because the quality of your leadership matters. Committing to learning and practicing leadership will definitely increase your capacity to have a more positive impact on those you lead and the larger community of which you are a part.

Fundamentals for Learning Leadership You don't need anyone's permission to become a better leader, nor are any spectacular resources required. Just as Dorothy and her colleagues in *The Wizard of Oz* discovered, you already have everything you need to exercise leadership. However, here are five fundamental strategies to follow on your yellow brick road to becoming the best leader you can be.[2]

Fundamental One: Believe You Can

No one is going to follow you for very long if you aren't willing to follow yourself. You have to believe that you can have a positive impact on others. Even if some people think that you're not able to learn leadership, *you* must believe that you can. That's where it all starts—with your own belief in yourself.

You have to believe that what you do counts. You have to believe that your words can inspire and your actions can move others. Believing that you can lead is essential to developing your leadership skills and abilities. If you don't believe this, it's unlikely that you will make any effort at all, let alone a sustained effort to become a better leader over time. No one can put leadership into you. You have to bring it out of yourself.

The best leaders have a growth mindset.[3] They believe that leadership is something that is learned and that they are capable of learning and developing throughout their lives. They also believe the same about others. Don't let anyone tell you that you don't make a difference or that others can't do the same. In these turbulent times there is no shortage of opportunities to lead, and the world needs more people who believe they can make a difference and who are willing to act on that belief.

Fundamental Two: Aspire to Excel

To become the very best leader you can be, you need to be clear about the core values and beliefs that guide your decisions and actions and about the vision you and others look forward to achieving. The same is true for learning leadership. You have to be clear about your motivations for wanting to be a leader. *Why* do you want to become a leader? Exactly what kind of a leader do you want to be?

Here's a hint: Your motivation needs to be intrinsic and not instrumental. Research has found that top-performing leaders don't focus on making money, getting a promotion, or being famous. They want to lead because they care deeply about the mission and people they are serving.[4]

Having a clear sense of mission and purpose also helps you continue your learning when times are particularly challenging.

Fundamental Three: Challenge Yourself

To develop as a leader and do your best, you have to step outside your comfort zone. You have to seek new experiences, test yourself, make some mistakes, and keep climbing back up that learning curve.

You have to be curious, taking the initiative to try new things and experimenting with new ideas and new ways of doing things. And when you do so, you are inevitably going to make mistakes and fail. The key is to draw lessons from the experience and repeating the cycle of learning.

To get better at leading, you also have to get gritty.[5] You have to persist in the face of difficulties; it means thinking more like a marathoner than a sprinter. Everyone stumbles in the process of developing, so don't let missteps sidetrack or dissuade you. Bounce forward from the setbacks. Strengthen your resilience.

Fundamental Four: Engage Support

You can't learn to become the best leader all by yourself. The top performers in every endeavor, including leaders, all seek out the support, advice, and counsel of others. That has a lot to do with why they turn out to be the most successful.

In the process of becoming more proficient in exercising leadership you need to make connections. You need those connections to be strong and personal, not simply transactional.[6] Connections open doors and can give you an opportunity to observe exemplary leadership up close and in action. You just have to take the initiative to create and sustain these relationships.

Fundamental Five: Practice Deliberately

You can't get any better at leadership without practice. Moreover, the time spent practicing won't amount to much unless you apply some discipline in this effort. Knowing your strengths and building upon them is important, but so is realizing that you are weak in some areas and addressing those.

Context significantly impacts your ability to grow and thrive as a leader. Environments of trust and respect are critical, as are opportunities for gaining new experiences, support for risk taking, and role models from whom you can learn. Sometimes you'll have the good fortune to work in those settings, and other times you'll have to take charge of creating your own culture of leadership development.

Being an exemplary leader requires a lifelong daily commitment to learning. No matter how many summits you've ascended, you have to take a step every day to improve—one reflection at a time, one question at a time, one lesson at a time. You have to commit to the habits of learning something new every day and the habit of assessing your progress every day. This perspective echoes what Jim Whittaker shared with us. Jim was the first American to summit Mt. Everest, the earth's highest mountain, and among his many other outdoor adventures, he twice captained his sailboat in the 2,400-mile Victoria-to-Maui International Yacht Race and made the 20,000-mile voyage from Washington to Australia four times. Upon reflecting on such adventures, he says that you have to make "the most of every moment, about stretching your own boundaries, about being willing to learn constantly, and putting yourself in situations where learning is possible."[7]

How People Learn to Lead

Our research has found that people who are most frequently engaged in learning, no matter what their learning style, also exercise leadership most frequently.[8] It has also been reported that those leaders who engage in learning for five or more hours per week, compared to those who spend an hour or less per week, are 74 percent more likely to have more direction in their careers and 48 percent more likely to find purpose in their work. They are also happier in the work.[9] The more you seek to learn, the better you will become at leadership (or at anything, for that matter). What's clear is that you have to approach each new and unfamiliar experience with a willingness to learn and an appreciation of the importance of learning.

We also discovered in our research that there is no one best way to learn. As part of the investigation into Personal-Best Leadership Experiences, people were asked, "How did you learn to lead?" Three major learning approaches emerged. The most frequent was through direct experiences, followed by observation and education.

Experience: Learning by Doing There's no substitute for learning by doing. Learning from trial and error—that "school of hard knocks" people talk about so often—is not just a saying. More people mentioned experience as the most important way to learn to lead than any other approach. Experience was mentioned almost twice as often as observation and nearly three times as often as education. The more chances you have to actually practice leadership in real-life situations, the more likely it is that you'll become better at it.

Whether it's facilitating team meetings, leading a special task force, heading a charity fundraising drive, or chairing a professional association's annual conference, the more chances you have to serve in leadership roles the more likely it is that you'll develop the skills to lead—and the more likely that you'll learn the important leadership lessons that come only from the failures and successes of action.

Just any experience, however, does not support individual development by itself. Challenge is crucial to learning and career enhancement. Boring, routine tasks don't help you improve your skills and abilities. You must stretch yourself. You must seek opportunities to test yourself against new and difficult tasks. Experience *can* indeed be the best teacher—if it includes the element of personal challenge. Whenever you select experiential activities to boost your performance, make sure you select projects and assignments that involve a stretch.[10] If you are put in a role that doesn't stretch you, figure out how to do it differently so that you *are* stretched and learning. Reflect on the lessons you learned that can be applied in future opportunities.

Example: Learning by Observing Others All the people around you are potential sources of learning. Role models are critical to learning, and they are especially important when learning how to lead. As you think about your continuing leadership development, look around for role models, coaches, and teachers in your organization or community. Don't be shy about asking for their help or for permission to watch them in action. Ask to sit in on meetings they run or attend presentations they make. Take them out to coffee and interview them on how they handle difficult situations. Ask them for feedback about how they may have seen you operate with your peers.

At work, the relationship that makes the most difference in your performance is the relationship you have with your immediate manager. Managers not only serve as potential role models, but they can also provide extremely useful developmental feedback. The best managers are those who challenge you, trust you, spend time with you, and teach you. If you are fortunate to have one of those managers who is a role model for leadership, take charge of this relationship and make the most of it. If you happen to have one of those managers who'd make a great candidate for the ten worst bosses, then observe what *not* to do. It's useful to be reminded that managers can have both a favorable and a damaging impact on others. Adopt the positive and reject the negative.

Peers are also valuable sources of knowledge, skill, and information. Trusted peers can serve as advisers and counselors, giving you feedback on your personal style and helping you test alternative ways of dealing with problems. If you have a colleague who's strong in an area in which you need to improve, ask that person to teach you what he or she knows. Ask people to share their best practices, and seek opportunities to observe them in action.

Education: Learning Through Training and Coursework

Formal training and coursework can definitely improve your leadership abilities. Even though people devote significantly less time to these, and the opportunities to participate and learn are often not as directly on-the-job or part of everyone's daily routines, they can still be a high-leverage opportunity. Done right, classes, workshops, and seminars enable you to spend a concentrated period of time with an expert focused on one subject and some specific skills. This concentrated attention helps you to learn something more quickly, with the benefit of having multiple chances to practice new behaviors and skills and obtain feedback in a safe environment.

Increasingly, as many people discovered during the coronavirus pandemic, you can do training on your own, through a plethora of online learning technologies featuring seminars, workshops, presentations, simulations, how-to sessions, threaded discussions, and the like. Whether it's sponsored by your organization or not, take advantage of self-directed learning opportunities that you can complete on your own time and at your own pace. In addition, consider picking up a couple of biographies of contemporary or historical people you admire and read about how they learned to lead, the struggles they dealt with and overcame.

Finally, to get the most out of any kind of educational experience, make sure you take the opportunity to apply what you've learned. In the leadership spirit, consider these to be "experiments." The probability that you'll apply what you've learned in training decreases with every day that passes that you don't do something new. Whenever possible, take the time as well to describe what you learned with your manager or colleagues because that's another effective method for taking an important first step in determining how to best apply what you learned or experienced in the classroom now that you are back "on the job."

Become Your Best Self

The instrument of leadership is the self, and mastery of the art of leadership comes from mastery of the self. While engineers have computers; painters, canvas and brushes; musicians, instruments; leaders have only themselves. *Leadership development is self-development*, and self-development is not simply about stuffing in a whole bunch of new information or trying out the latest technique. It's about leading out of the potential you already have. It's about liberating the leader within. The quest for leadership is first an inner quest to discover who you are. Seeing yourself as a leader, and exercising leadership more often, will fundamentally change who you are.

You're no longer an individual contributor. You're now someone who takes people on journeys to places they've never been.

Thinking about yourself as a leader changes you.

- ▶ It changes how you present yourself day in and day out. You are expected to be a role model for the values that you and the organization espouse.

- ▶ It changes how you see the future. You are expected to be able to imagine exciting future possibilities and communicate them to others.

- ▶ It changes how you respond to challenges. You are expected to be comfortable with uncertainty, champion experimentation, and learn from experiences.

- ▶ It changes how you relate to others. You are expected to build relationships, foster collaboration, strengthen those around you, and forge trust.

- ▶ It changes how you show others that you appreciate them. You are expected to sincerely recognize contributions and celebrate team successes.

Being true to these expectations and leading with your best self means that you need to be clear and comfortable with the kind of leader you want to become.

Start the journey to become the best leader you can be by envisioning how you want to be a leader in the future. Kick-start that conversation with yourself by imaging the following scenario:

> It's ten years from today, and you are attending a ceremony honoring you as the "Leader of the Year." One after another, colleagues and co-workers, members of your family, and good friends take the stage and talk about your leadership and how you have made a positive difference in their lives.
>
> To help you think about what you hope people will say about you that day and how you would hope to be remembered, record your responses to this L.I.F.E. paradigm:

Lessons: What vital *lessons* do you hope others will say you have passed on? (For example: She taught me how to face adversity with grace and determination. He taught me the importance of giving back to those who've given to you.)

Ideals: What *ideals*—values, principles, and ethical standards—do you hope people will say you stand for? (For example: She stands for freedom and justice. He believes in always telling the truth, even when it isn't what people want to hear.)

Feelings: What *feelings* do you hope people will say they have or had when being with you or when thinking about you? (For example: She always made me feel I was capable of doing the impossible. He made me feel important.)

Evidence: What is the *evidence* that you made a difference; what lasting *expressions* or contributions—tangible and intangible—will people say that you leave to them and to others yet to come? (For example: She is really the one who turned this organization around. His dedication to others lives on in those homes that he helped us build and design.)

The next step, after you've written down your responses to the above, is to ask yourself: How am I doing right now in teaching these *lessons*, living up to these *ideals*, creating these *feelings*, and providing the *evidence* that I am contributing as a leader? Then ask yourself: What can I do to do better? The likelihood of that ceremony ever happening in the future begins with how you behave right now.

Our Aspiration for You

"It's not very difficult to find examples of The Five Practices evident in my workplace and in my personal life," Natraj Iyer, responsible for business development at an AI-based product research firm, wrote to us when he completed The Leadership Challenge® Workshop. We certainly agree, but we were even more struck by another of his observations: "We often think of leadership as something big and grand, but based on my experiences, I think real leadership is everywhere and in the daily moments. We all have several opportunities in our daily lives to seize the moment and be the leaders we can be. Each and every one of us has a choice to be that leader. We can listen to our hearts and seize the moment, or let it go by."

He's nailed it. You have to say "yes" when the opportunity presents itself. Nothing happens unless you say yes. In order to improve your leadership abilities, you have to say yes to starting new things. You have to say yes to your beliefs, to difficult challenges, to collaboration, to trust, to setting an example, to learning, and you have to say yes to your heart. When you are ready to say yes, doors will open to entirely new adventures in your life and prospects for making a difference.

Our wish is that you make the most of every opportunity you have to lead, that you stretch yourself and be willing to learn continually from the challenges in front of you, and that you step out to the edge of your capabilities—and then ask a little bit more of yourself.

APPENDIX: THE RESEARCH BASIS FOR THIS BOOK

THE PRINCIPLES AND practices described in this book are based solidly in both qualitative and quantitative research studies. Responses from more than 29,000 people provided a robust sample for completing statistical analyses showing that the exercise of leadership positively impacted their workplace attitudes and effectiveness assessments.

The respondents for this book's empirical analysis completed the Observer form of the LPI, indicating that they were a colleague or co-worker of an individual who completed the LPI–Self. All of the Self-respondents in this analysis identified themselves as an "individual contributor" rather than in a hierarchical or management position. The data was collected over three years—between January 2017 and December 2019. Peer assessments are particularly valuable because they avoid self-report bias, are considered more objective than subjective, and have been shown as most robust in predicting key behavioral and organizational outcomes for others, such as the potential for career derailment and productivity.[1]

The demographic characteristics of the co-workers and colleagues in this sample were very similar to those individual contributors (their peers) who completed the LPI–Self. They were typically from the United States (82 percent), female (53 percent), between the ages of 24 and 49 (70 percent), and had earned at least a college degree (83 percent). Twenty-seven percent had been with their current employer for less than three years, 36 percent three-to-ten years, and 37 percent for more than ten years. They were employed across a variety of industries (e.g., finance and banking, retail, medical/health care, government, manufacturing, social services, military, pharmaceuticals, high technology, and telecommunications) and functional areas (e.g., operations, engineering, finance, sales, IT, marketing, and R&D). About 19 percent of the organizations employed fewer than 100 people, 19 percent employed 100 to 499 people, 11 percent employed 500 to 999 people, 27 percent employed 1,000 to 9,999, and 24 percent employed more than 10,000 people. It should be noted that demographic differences have generally not been shown to impact the relationships between assessments of leader behavior and various measures of engagement.

In addition to providing demographic information, respondents had the option of answering a series of other questions. They were asked about the extent to which they agreed or disagreed with statements concerning how they felt about their workplace. For example: "I feel that my organization values my work" and "I care about the long-term success of the organization." In addition, they were asked about the extent to which they agreed or disagreed with statements evaluating the effectiveness of the individual who had asked them to provide feedback. "Overall, this person is an effective leader" and "I feel valued by this person" are examples of these statements. A five-point Likert scale using "1" Strongly

---

[1]Braddy, P.W., Gooty, J., Fleenor, J.W., and Yammarino, F.J. "Leader Behaviors and Career Derailment Potential: A Multi-Analytic Method Examination of Rating Source and Self-Other Agreement," *The Leadership Quarterly*, 2014, 25(2), 373–390.

disagree, "2" Disagree, "3" Neither agree nor disagree, "4" Agree, and "5" Strongly agree were used for these statements and assessments.

Pearson's chi-squared tests and analysis of variance (ANOVA) were the two dominant statistical tools used in the analyses. Probabilities were set at $p < .001$ for determining the likelihood that such a relationship or difference would be the result of chance. All the data analyses presented in this book met or exceeded this probability threshold, lending strong empirical support to the claim that engaging in The Five Practices of Exemplary Leadership makes a difference.

Leadership matters, and so do you. The research clearly shows that exercising leadership doesn't require your being in some special position or function, or location in your organization. We believe that you are already leading, just possibly not frequently enough or with sufficient intentionality and self-awareness. We know that your effectiveness as a leader is tied to the frequency with which you Model the Way, Inspire a Shared Vision, Challenge the Process, Enable Others to Act, and Encourage the Heart. In this book, we have provided the way, and now you have to provide the willingness to become the best leader you can be.

ENDNOTES

Chapter 1:
Leadership Is Not a Position

1. McGirt, Ellen. "World's 50 greatest leaders," *Fortune*, April 18, 2019. Accessed on March 18, 2020. https://fortune.com/worlds-greatest-leaders/2019/search/
2. "New class: The Forum of Young Global Leaders." The Forum of Young Global Leaders. Accessed on March 18, 2020. https://www.younggloballeaders.org/new-class
3. Posner, B.Z. "When It Comes to Leadership, Who Are the Role Models?" Working paper, Leavey School of Business, Santa Clara University, 2020.
4. Posner, B.Z. "The Influence of Demographic Factors on What People Want from Their Leaders," *Journal of Leadership Studies*, 2018, 12(2), 7–16.
5. Hovland, C.I., Janis, I.I., and Kelley, H.H. *Communication and Persuasion.* New Haven, CT: Yale University Press, 1953. Also see Cialdini, R. *Influence: The Psychology of Persuasion.* New York: Collins, 2007.
6. Kouzes, J.M., and Posner, B.Z. *Credibility: How Leaders Gain and Lose It, Why People Demand It* (2nd ed.). Hoboken, NJ: The Leadership Challenge—A Wiley Brand, 2011.

7.   See, for example: Caza, A., Caza, B., and Posner, B.Z. "Transformational Leadership in Cultural Context: Follower Perception and Satisfaction," Working paper, Leavey School of Business, Santa Clara University, 2020; Caza, A., and Posner, B.Z. "The Influence of Nationality on Followers' Satisfaction with Their Leaders," *Journal of Leadership, Accountability, and Ethics,* 2017, 14(3), 53–62.

8.   For more information about these studies, you can find abstracts of over 800 of them on our website: https://www.leadershipchallenge.com /research/others-research.aspx. Also see Posner, B.Z. "Bringing the Rigor of Research to the Art of Leadership: Evidence Behind The Five Practices of Exemplary Leadership and the LPI: Leadership Practices Inventory." http://www.leadershipchallenge.com/LeadershipChallenge/media /SiteFiles/research/our-research/tlc-our-research-bringing-the-rigor-of -research-to-the-art-of-leadership.pdf

9.   Kouzes, J.M., and Posner, B.Z. *The Leadership Challenge: How to Make Extraordinary Things Happen in Organizations* (6th ed.). Hoboken, NJ: The Leadership Challenge—A Wiley Brand, 2017.

10. Kouzes, J.M., and Posner, B.Z. *LPI: Leadership Practices Inventory* (45th ed.). Hoboken, NJ: The Leadership Challenge—A Wiley Brand, 2017. https://www.leadershipchallenge.com/LeadershipChallenge/media/ SiteFiles/resources/sample-reports/tlc-lpi-360-english-v5.pdf

11. For more information about these studies, see our website: https://www. leadershipchallenge.com/research/others-research.aspx

Chapter 2: Model the Way

1.   Lamott, A. *Bird by Bird: Some Instructions on Writing and Life.* New York: Pantheon, 1994, pp. 199–200.

2.   For example, see: Buller, J.L. *Positive Academic Leadership: How to Stop Putting Out Fires and Start Making a Difference.* San Francisco: Jossey-Bass, 2013; Gentry, W.A., and Sparks, T.E. "A Convergence/Divergence Perspective of Leadership Competencies Managers Believe Are Most Important for Success in Organizations: A Cross-Cultural Multilevel Analysis of 40 Countries," *Journal of Business and Psychology,* 2012, 27(1), 15–30.

3. Daniels, C. "Developing Organizational Values in Others." In Crandall, D. (ed.), *Leadership Lessons from West Point*. San Francisco: Jossey-Bass, 2007, 62–87; Rhoads, A., and Shepherdson, N. *Build on Values: Creating an Enviable Culture That Outperforms the Competition*. San Francisco: Jossey-Bass, 2011.

4. Posner, B.Z. "Another Look at the Impact of Personal and Organizational Values Congruency," *Journal of Business Ethics*, 2010, 97(4), 535–541.

5. Schein, E., with Schein, P. *Organizational Culture and Leadership* (5th ed.). Hoboken, NJ: Wiley, 2017.

6. Callahan, S. *Putting Stories to Work: Mastering Business Storytelling*. Melbourne: Pepperberg Press, 2016.

7. As quoted in Schawbel, D. "How to Use Storytelling as a Leadership Tool," *Forbes*, April 13, 2012. http://www.forbes.com/sites /danschawbel/2012/08/13/how-to-use-storytelling-as-a-leadership -tool/#3fdcf5277ac9

8. For example, see Denning, S. *The Secret Language of Leadership: How Leaders Inspire Action Through Narrative*. San Francisco: Jossey-Bass, 2007; Wortmann, C. *What's Your Story? Using Stories to Ignite Performance and Be More Successful*. Chicago: Kaplan, 2006; Zak, P.J. "Why Your Brain Loves Good Storytelling," *Harvard Business Review*, October 28, 2014. https://hbr.org/2014/10/why-your-brain-loves-good-storytelling; Martin, S.R. "Stories About Values and Valuable Stories: A Field Experiment of the Power of Narratives to Shape Newcomers' Actions," *Academy of Management Journal*, 2016, 59(5), 1707–1724.

9. Blanchard, F.A., Lilly, T., and Vaughn, L.A. "Reducing the Expression of Racial Prejudice," *Psychological Science*, 1991, 2(2), 101–105.

10. Rosso, B.D., Dekas, K.H., and Wrzeniewski, A. "On the Meaning of Work: A Theoretical Integration and Review," *Research in Organizational Behavior*, 2010, 30, 91–127.

11. Zuboff, S. *In the Age of the Smart Machine: The Future of Work and Power*. New York: Basic Books, 1988, p. 394.

12. Newberg, A., and Waldman, M.R. *Words Can Change Your Brain: 12 Conversation Strategies to Build Trust, Resolve Conflict, and Increase Intimacy*. New York: Penguin, 2012, p. 7.

13. Brooks, A.W., and John, L.K. "The Surprising Power of Questions," *Harvard Business Review*, May-June 2018, pp. 60–67.

14. Brooks and John, loc cit., p. 64.

15. Huang, K., Yeomans, M., Brooks, A.W., Minson, J., and Gino, F. "It Doesn't Hurt to Ask: Question-Asking Increases Liking." *Journal of Personality and Social Psychology*, 2017, 113(3), 430–452.

16. As quoted in Brooks and John, loc. cit., p. 65.

17. Stone, D., and Heen, S. *Thanks for the Feedback: The Science and Art of Receiving Feedback Well.* New York: Penguin, 2015.

18. Gino, F. "Research: We Drop People Who Give Us Critical Feedback," *Harvard Business Review*, September 16, 2016. https://hbr.org/2016/09 /research-we-drop-people-who-give-us-critical-feedback

19. Zenger, J. "There Is No Feedback Fallacy: Understanding the Value of Feedback," May 13, 2019. https://www.forbes.com/sites/jackzenger /2019/05/13/there-is-no-feedback-fallacy-understanding-the-value-of -feedback/#3da55df15368

20. Yoon, J., Blunden, H., Kristal, A., and Whillans, A. "Why Asking for Advice Is More Effective Than Asking for Feedback," *Harvard Business Review*, September 20, 2019. https://hbr.org/2019/09/why-asking-for -advice-is-more-effective-than-asking-for-feedback

Chapter 3: Inspire a Shared Vision

1. We are grateful to Dan Schwab for sharing this example.

2. Bailey, C., and Madden, A. "What Makes Work Meaningful—or Meaningless," *MIT Sloan Management Review*, 2016, 67(1), 52–61.

3. Hurst, A., and others. *Purpose at Work: 2016 Global Report.* LinkedIn and Imperative. Accessed on 3/24/20. https://business.linkedin.com/content /dam/me/business/en-us/talent-solutions/resources/pdfs/purpose-at -work-global-report.pdf

4. Lucas, A.F. "A Teamwork Approach to Change in the Academic Department." In Lucas, A.F., and Associates, *Leading Academic Change* (pp. 7–32). San Francisco: Jossey-Bass, 2000.

5. Palmer, P.J. *Let Your Life Speak: Listening for the Voice of Vocation.* San Francisco: Jossey-Bass, 2000.

6. Hurst, A., and others. "Purpose at Work: The Largest Global Study on the Role of Purpose in the Workforce," 2016. https://cdn.imperative.com /media/public/Global_Purpose_Index_2016.pdf

7. Newton, J., and Davis, J. "Three Secrets of Organizational Success," *Strategy+Business,* 2014, Autumn (76); also see Sinek, S. *Start with Why: How Great Leaders Inspire Everyone to Take Action.* New York: Portfolio, 2010.

8. Goleman, D. *Social Intelligence: The New Science of Human Relationships.* New York: Bantam, 2006.

9. Fredrickson, B.L. *Positivity: Groundbreaking Research Reveals How to Embrace the Hidden Strengths of Positive Emotions, Overcome Negativity, and Thrive.* New York: Crown Publishers, 2009.

10. Bass, B.M. *Leadership and Performance Beyond Expectations.* New York: Free Press, 1985, p. 35.

11. Halpren, B.L., and Lubar, K. *Leadership Presence: Dramatic Techniques to Reach Out, Motivate, and Inspire.* New York: Gotham Books, 2003.

12. Van Edwards, V. "5 Secrets of a Successful Ted Talk" Last modified December 6, 2017. https://www.huffpost.com/entry/5-secrets-of-a -successful_b_6887472

13. Koppensteiner, M., Stephan, P., and Jaschke, J.P.M. "From Body Motion to Cheers: Speakers' Body Movements as Predictors of Applause," *Personality and Individual Differences,* 2015, 74, 182–185.

Chapter 4: Challenge the Process

1. We are grateful to Steve Coats for sharing this example.

2. Crant, M.J., and Bateman, T.S. "Charismatic Leadership Viewed from Above: The Impact of Proactive Personality," *Journal of Organizational Behavior,* 2000, 21(1), 63–75.

3. Crant, M.J., and Bateman, T.S. "The Proactive Component of Organizational Behavior: Measures and Correlates," *Journal of Organizational Behavior,* 1993, 14, 103–118; Crant, J.M. "Proactive Behavior in Organizations," *Journal of Management,* 2000, 26(3), 435–463.

4. See, for example: Crant, J.M. "The Proactive Personality Scale and Objective Job Performance Among Real Estate Agents," *Journal of Applied Psychology,* 1995, 80(4), 532–537; Seibert, E., and Braimer, M.L. "What Do Proactive People Do? A Longitudinal Model Linking Proactive Personality and Career Success," *Personnel Psychology,* 2001, 54, 845–875; Thompson,

J.A. "Proactive Personality and Job Performance: A Social Capital Perspective," *Journal of Applied Psychology,* 2005, 90(5), 1011–1017; Brown, D.J., Cober, R.T., Kane, K., Levy, P.E., and Shalhoop, J. "Proactive Personality and the Successful Job Search: A Field Investigation of College Graduates," *Journal of Applied Psychology,* 2006, 91(3), 717–726; Kim, T-Y, Hon, A.H.Y., and Crant, J.M. "Proactive Personality, Employee Creativity, and Newcomer Outcomes: A Longitudinal Study," *Journal of Business and Psychology,* 2009, 24(1), 93–103; Li, N., Liang, J., and Crant, J.M. "The Role of Proactive Personality in Job Satisfaction and Organizational Citizenship Behavior: A Relational Perspective," *Journal of Applied Psychology,* 2010, 95(2), 395–404; Spitzmuller, M., Sin, H-P, Howe, M., and Fatimah, S. "Investigating the Uniqueness and Usefulness of Proactive Personality in Organizational Research: A Meta-Analytic Review," *Human Performance,* 2015, 28(4), 351–379.

5. Deci, E.L. *Intrinsic Motivation.* New York: Plenum Press, 1975; Pink, D.H. *Drive: The Surprising Truth About What Motivates Us.* New York: Riverhead Books, 2011.

6. Csikszentmihalyi, M. *Flow: The Psychology of Optimal Experience.* New York: Harper & Row, 1990.

7. Csikszentmihalyi, M. *Beyond Boredom and Anxiety: The Experience of Play in Work and Games.* San Francisco: Jossey-Bass, 1975, p. 30.

8. Wheatley, M. *Leadership and the New Science.* San Francisco: Berrett-Koehler, 1992.

9. Nicolini, D., Korica, M., and Ruddle, K. "Staying in the Know," *Sloan Management Review,* 2015, 56(4), 57–65.

10. See, for example: Katz, R. "The Influence of Group Longevity: High Performance Research Teams," *Wharton Magazine,* 1982, 6(3), 28–34; Katz, R., and Allen, T.J. "Investigating the Not Invented Here (NIH) Syndrome: A Look at the Performance, Tenure, and Communication Patterns of 50 R&D Project Groups." In Tushman, M.L., and Moore, W.L. (eds.), *Readings in the Management of Innovation* (2nd ed.). Cambridge: Ballinger Publishing Company, 1988, pp. 293–309; Tushman, M.L., and O'Reilly, C.A. *Winning Through Innovation: A Practical Guide to Leading Organizational Change and Renewal* (rev. ed.). Cambridge: Harvard Business Review Press, 2002.

11. Brooks, A. W., Gino, F., and Schweitzer, M.E. "Smart People Ask for (My) Advice: Seeking Advice Boosts Perceptions of Competence," *Management Science,* 2015, 61(6), 1421–1435.

12. Berns, G. *Iconoclast: A Neuroscientist Reveals How to Think Differently.* Cambridge, MA: Harvard Business School Press, 2008.

13. Christensen, C., Dyer, J., and Gregersen, H. "The Innovator's DNA," *Harvard Business Review,* 2009, 87(2), 60–67.

14. Sims, P. *Little Bets: How Breakthrough Ideas Emerge from Small Discoveries.* New York: Free Press, 2011, 141–152.

15. Fogg, B.J. *Tiny Habits: The Small Changes That Change Everything.* New York: Houghton Mifflin Harcourt, 2020; also see Clear, J. *Atomic Habits: An Easy & Proven Way to Build Good Habits & Break Bad Ones.* New York: Penguin Random House, 2018.

16. Thaler, R.H., and Sunstein, C.R. *Nudge: Improving Decisions About Health, Wealth, and Happiness.* New York: Penguin Books, 2009.

17. Edmondson, A.C. *The Fearless Organization: Creating Psychological Safety in the Workplace for Learning, Innovation, and Growth.* Hoboken, NJ: Wiley, 2019.

18. Rock, D. "Managing with the Brain in Mind," *Strategy + Business.* Last modified August 27, 2009. https://www.strategy-business.com /article/09306?gko=5df7f

19. Kahnerman, D. *Thinking, Fast and Slow.* New York: Farrar, Strauss and Giroux, 2011.

20. Edmondson, Ibid.

21. Duhigg, C. "What Google Learned from Its Quest to Build the Perfect Team," *The New York Times Magazine.* Last modified February 25, 2016. https://www.nytimes.com/2016/02/28/magazine/what-google-learned -from-its-quest-to-build-the-perfect-team.html

22. O.C. Tanner Institute. 2020 Global Culture Report. Salt Lake City, UT, p. 2.

23. Schein, E.H. *Humble Inquiry: The Gentle Art of Asking Instead of Telling.* San Francisco, CA: Berrett-Koehler, 2013.

24. Edmonson, op. cit., p. 200.

25. Weick, K.E. "Small Wins: Redefining the Scale of Social Problems," *American Psychologist*, 1984, 39(1), 40–49.

26. Amabile, T.A., and Kramer, S.J. *The Progress Principle: Using Small Wins to Ignite Joy, Engagement, and Creativity at Work.* Boston: Harvard Business Review Press, 2011, p. 75.

27. Dahle, C. "Natural Leader," *Fast Company,* December 2000, 270–280; Schoemaker, P.J., and Cunther, R.E. "The Wisdom of Deliberate Mistakes," *Harvard Business Review*, June 2006, 108–115.

28. Eisenstadt, K.M., and Tabrizi, B.N. "Accelerating Adaptive Processes: Product Innovation in the Global Computer Industry," *Administrative Science Quarterly*, 1995, 40, 84–110; Williams, E., and Shaffer, A.R. "The Defense Innovation Initiative: The Importance of Capability Prototyping," *Joint Force Quarterly*, 2015, 2nd Quarter, 34–43.

29. Harford, T. *Adapt: Why Success Always Starts with Failure*. New York: Picador, 2012.

30. Schoemaker, P.J., and Cunther, R.E. "The Wisdom of Deliberate Mistakes," *Harvard Business Review*, June 2006, 108–115.

31. Bayles, D., and Orland, T. *Art and Fear: Observations on the Perils (and Rewards) of Artmaking*. Eugene, OR: Image Continuum Press, 2001.

32. Kouzes, J.M., and Posner, B.Z. *The Truth About Leadership: The No-Fads, Heart-of-the-Matter Facts You Need to Know*. San Francisco: Jossey-Bass, 2010, 119–135.

33. Dalton, M., Swigert, S., Van Velsor, E., Bunker, E., and Wachholz, J. *The Learning Tactics Inventory: Facilitator's Guide*. San Francisco: Jossey-Bass, 1999.

34. Dweck, C.S. *Mindset: The New Psychology of Success*. New York: Random House, 2006.

35. Bandura, A., and Wood, R.E. "Effects of Perceived Controllability and Performance Standards on Self-Regulation of Complex Decision Making," *Journal of Personality and Social Psychology,* 1989, 56, 805–814. Also see: Dweck, C.S. *Mindset*. New York: Random House, 2006; Ericsson, A., and Pool, R. *Peak: Secrets from the New Science of Expertise*. New York: Houghton Mifflin Harcourt, 2016.

36. Kouzes, T.K., and Posner, B.Z. "Influence of Mindset on Leadership Behavior," *Leadership & Organization Development Journal*, 2019, 40(8), 829–844.

37. McKnight, K.A. *The Resilience Way: Overcome the Unexpected and Build an Extraordinary Life . . . on Your Own Terms!* Independently published, 2019.

38. Shatte, A., and Bruce, J. *The Science Behind Resilience: A Study of Psychometric Measures & Business Outcomes,* meQuilibrium, 2015. https://euev9yjpvg1o6bsamcfdw11x-wpengine.netdna-ssl.com/wpcontent/uploads/2016/01/The-Science-Behind-Resilience-12-22.pdf

39. Duckworth, A.L., Peterson, C., Matthews, M.D., and Kelly, D.R. "Grit: Perseverance and Passion for Long-Term Goals," *Journal of Personality*

and Social Psychology, 2007, 92(6), 1087–1101. Also see Duckworth, A.L. *Grit: The Power of Passion and Perseverance.* New York: Scribner, 2016.

40.   Caza, A., and Posner, B.Z. "How and When Does Grit Influence Leaders' Behavior?" *Leadership & Organization Development Journal,* 2019, 40(1), 124–134; Caza, A., and Posner, B.Z. "An Exploratory Investigation into How Grit Influences the Leadership Practices of Sales Managers," *Journal of Selling,* 2019, 19(2), 36–45.

41.   See Salvatore, S.R. "The Story of Hardiness: Twenty Years of Theorizing, Research, and Practice," *Consulting Psychology Journal: Practices and Research,* 2002, 54(3), 175–185. Also see: Maddi, S.R., and Kobasa, S.C. *The Hardy Executive: Health Under Stress.* Chicago: Dorsey Press, 1984; Maddi, S.R., and Khoshaba, D.M. *Resilience at Work: How to Succeed No Matter What Life Throws at You.* New York: AMACOM, 2005.

42.   For example, see Bartone, P.T. "Resilience Under Military Operational Stress: Can Leaders Influence Hardiness?" *Military Psychology,* 2006, 18, S141–S148; Bruce, R.A., and Sinclair, R.F. "Exploring the Psychological Hardiness of Entrepreneurs," *Frontiers of Entrepreneurship Research* 2009, 29(6), 5; Bartone, P.T. "Social and Organizational Influences on Psychological Hardiness: How Leaders Can Increase Stress Resilience," *Security Informatics,* 2012, 1, 1–10; Sandvik, A.M., Hansena, A.L., Hystada, S.W., Johnsena, B.H., and Barton, P.T. "Psychopathy, Anxiety, and Resiliency—Psychological Hardiness as a Mediator of the Psychopathy–Anxiety Relationship in a Prison Setting," *Personality and Individual Differences,* 2015, 72, 30–34.

43.   Smith, E.S. "On Coronavirus Lockdown? Look for Meaning, Not Happiness," *New York Times.* Last modified April 7, 2020. https://nyti.ms/2wjAVddy

44.   We are grateful to Valarie Willis for sharing this example.

Chapter 5: Enable Others to Act

1.   We are grateful to Valarie Willis for sharing this example.

2.   Gurtman, M.B. "Trust, Distrust, and Interpersonal Problems: A Circumplex Analysis," *Journal of Personality and Social Psychology,* 1992, 62, 989–1002; Grace, G.D., and Schill, T. "Social Support and Coping

Endnotes

Style Differences in Subjects High and Low in Interpersonal Trust," *Psychological Reports*, 1986, 59, 584–586.

3. Driscoll, J.W. "Trust and Participation in Organizational Decision Making as Predictors of Satisfaction," *Academy of Management Journal*, 1978, 21(1), 44–56.

4. Shockley-Zalabak, P.S., Morreale, S., and Hackman, M. *Building the High-Trust Organization: Strategies for Supporting Five Key Dimensions of Trust.* San Francisco: Jossey-Bass, 2010.

5. Zenger, J., and Folkman, J. "What Great Listeners Actually Do," *Harvard Business Review*, July 14, 2016.

6. Ibid.

7. Poundstone, W. *Prisoner's Dilemma: John Von Neumann, Game Theory, and the Puzzle of the Bomb.* New York: Doubleday, 1992.

8. Axelrod, R. *The Evolution of Cooperation* (rev. ed.). New York: Basic Books, 2006.

9. Flynn, F.J. "How Much Should I Give and How Often? The Effects of Generosity and Frequency of Favor Exchange on Social Status and Productivity," *Academy of Management Journal*, 2003, 46(5), 539–553.

10. Cialdini, R.B. *Influence: Science and Practice* (4th ed.). Needham Heights, MA: Allyn and Bacon, 2001; Melamed, D., Simpson, B., and Abernathy, J. "The Robustness of Reciprocity: Experimental Evidence That Each Form of Reciprocity Is Robust in the Presence of Other Forms of Reciprocity," *Science Advances*, 2020, 6(23). eaba0504. DOI:10.1126/sciadv.aba0504

11. Grant, A. *Give and Take: Why Helping Others Drives Our Success.* New York: Penguin Group, 2013.

12. Johnson, M.D., Hollenbeck, J.R., Humphrey, S.E., Ilgen, D.R., Jundt, D., and Meyer, C.J. "Cutthroat Cooperation: Asymmetrical Adaptation to Changes in Team Reward Structures," *Academy of Management Journal*, 2006, 49(1), 103–119.

13. See, for example: Baker, W. *Achieving Success Through Social Capital: Tapping the Hidden Resources in Your Personal and Business Networks.* San Francisco: Jossey-Bass, 2000; Powdthavve, N. "Putting a Price Tag on Friends, Relatives, and Neighbours: Using Surveys of Life Satisfaction to Value Social Relationships," *The Journal of Socio-Economics*, 2004, 37(4), 1459–1480.

14. Davidov, M., Zahn-Waxler, C., Roth-Hanania, R., and Knafo, A. "Concern for Others in the First Year of Life: Theory, Evidence, and Avenues for Research," *Child Development Perspectives*, 2013, *7*(2), 126–131.

15. See, for example: Bohns, V.K., and Flynn, F.J. "'Why Didn't You Just Ask?' Understanding the Discomfort of Help-Seeking," *Journal of Experimental Social Psychology*, 2010, 46(2), 402–409; DePaulo, B.M., and Fisher, J.D. "The Costs of Asking for Help," *Basic and Applied Social Psychology*, 2010, 1(1), 23–35.

16. See, for example: Dutton, J.E. "Building High-Quality Connections." In Dutton, J.E., and Spreitzer, G. (eds.), *How to Be a Positive Leader: Small Actions, Big Impact*. San Francisco: Berrett-Koehler, 2014, pp. 11–21; Clausen, T., Christensen, K.B., and Nielsen, K. "Does Group-Level Commitment Predict Employee Well-Being?" *Journal of Occupational and Environmental Medicine*, 2015, 57(11), 1141–1146.

17. Spataro, J. "What Generation Z Wants from Leaders." Last modified August 14, 2019. Development Dimensions International, Inc. https://www.ddiworld.com/blog/what-generation-z-wants-from-leaders

18. Baumeister, R.F., and Leary, M.R. "The Need to Belong: Desire for Interpersonal Attachments as a Fundamental Human Motivation," *Psychological Bulletin*, 1995, 117, 479–529.

19. Thackray, J. "Feedback for Real," *Gallup Management Journal,* Spring 2001, 1(1), 12–17; Gallup. *State of the Global Workplace*. New York: Gallup Press, 2017.

20. Williams, S.R., and Wilson, R.L. "Group Support Systems, Power, and Influence in an Organization—a Field Study," *Decision Sciences,* 1997, 28(4), 911–937; Azzarello, P. "Why Sharing Power at Work Is the Very Best Way to Build It, " *Fast Company*, January 18, 2013. https://www.fastcompany.com/3004867/why-sharing-power-work-very-best-way-build-it; Deci, E.L., Olafsen, A.H., and Ryan, R.M. "Self-Determination Theory in Work Organizations: The State of a Science," *Annual Review of Organizational Psychology and Organization Behavior*, 1017, 4, 19–43. https://doi.org/10.1146/annurev-orgpsych-032516-113108

21. Delgado, M.R. "Reward-Related Responses in the Human Striatum," *Annals of the New York Academy of Science,* 2007, 1104, 70–88; Fareri, D.S., Martin, L.N., and Delgado, M.R. "Reward-Related Processing in the Human Brain: Developmental Considerations," *Development & Psychopathology,* 2008, 20(4), 1191–1211; Delgado, M.R., Carson, M.M., and

Phelps, E.A. "Regulating the Expectation of Reward," *Nature Neuroscience,* 2008, 11(8), 880–881.

22. Psychologists often refer to this as self-efficacy. See, for example, Bandura, A. *Self-Efficacy: The Exercise of Control.* New York: Freeman, 1997; Maddux, J.E. "Self-Efficacy: The Power of Believing You Can." In Lopez, S.J., and Snyder, C.R. (eds.), *The Oxford Handbook of Positive Psychology* (2nd ed.). New York: Oxford University Press, 2011, 335–344.

23. Wood, R., and Bandura, A. "Impact of Conceptions of Ability on Self-Regulatory Mechanisms and Complex Decision Making," *Journal of Personality and Social Psychology,* 1989, 56, 407–415.

24. Leone, P. "Take Your ROI to Level 6," *Training Industry Quarterly*, Spring 2008, 14–18. http://www.nxtbook.com/nxtbooks/trainingindustry /tiq_2008spring/

25. Nawaz, S. "To Get Promoted, Get Feedback from Your Critics," *Harvard Business Review*, November 10, 2016. https://hbr.org/2016/11 /to-get-promoted-get-feedback-from-your-critics?referral=00203&utm _source=newsletter_management_tip&utm_medium=email& utm _campaign=tip_date; Barrington, L. "Everyone Needs a Personal Board of Directors," *Forbes*. Last modified February 20, 2018. https://www. forbes.com/sites/forbescoachescouncil/2018/02/20/everyone-needs-a -personal-board-of-directors/#4d39dd642bbc. Also see Kouzes, J.M., and Posner, B.Z. *Learning Leadership: The Five Fundamentals of Becoming an Exemplary Leader*. Hoboken, NJ: The Leadership Challenge—A Wiley Brand, 2016.

26. Gino, F. "Research: We Drop People Who Give Us Critical Feedback," *Harvard Business Review*. Last modified September 16, 2016. https://hbr .org/2016/09/research-we-drop-people-who-give-us-critical-feedback

Chapter 6: Encourage the Heart

1. See: Martin, S., and Marks, J. *Messengers: Who We Listen To, Who We Don't, and Why.* New York: Hachette Book Group, 2008; Cuddy, A.J., Fiske, S.T., and Glick, P. "Warmth and Competence as Universal Dimensions of Social Perception: The Stereotype Content Model and the BIAS Map," *Advances in Experimental Social Psychology*, 2019, 40, 61–149.

Endnotes

2. Van Kleef, G.A., De Dreu, C.K., and Manstead, A.S. "An Interpersonal Approach to Emotion in Social Decision Making: The Emotions as Social Information Model," *Advances in Experimental Social Psychology*, 2010, 42, 45–96.

3. Smith, A.E., Jussim, L., Eccles, J., VanNoy, M., Madon, S., and Palumbo, P. "Self-Fulfilling Prophecies, Perceptual Biases, and Accuracy at the Individual and Group Levels," *Journal of Experimental Social Psychology*, 1998, 34(6), 530–561; Eden, D. "Leadership and Expectations: Pygmalion Effects and Other Self-Fulfilling Prophecies in Organizations," *The Leadership Quarterly*, 1992, 3(4), 271–305.

4. Blitzer, R.J., Petersen, C., and Rogers, L. "How to Build Self-Esteem," *Training and Development Journal*, February. 1993, p. 59.

5. Cameron, K.S. *Positive Leadership: Strategies for Extraordinary Performance*. San Francisco: Berrett-Koehler, 2008.

6. Cooperrider, D.L. "Positive Image, Positive Action: The Affirmative Basis of Organizing." In Srivastva, S., Cooperrider, D.L., and Associates (eds.), *Appreciative Management and Leadership: The Power of Positive Thought and Action in Organizations*. San Francisco: Jossey-Bass, 1990, p. 103.

7. Cooperrider, loc. cit., p. 114.

8. Shaiar, J. "The State of Employee Engagement in 2016," November 1, 2016, https://www.business2community.com/human-resources/state-employee -engagement-2016-01695227.

9. McCarty, P.A. "Effects of Feedback on the Self-Confidence of Men and Women," *Academy of Management Journal*, 1986, 29(4), 840–847.

10. Ross, J.A. "Does Friendships Improve Job Performance?" *Harvard Business Review*, March-April 1977, 8–9; Jehn, K.A., and Shah, P.P. "Interpersonal Relationships and Task Performance: An Examination of Mediating Processes in Friendship and Acquaintance Groups," *Journal of Personality and Social Psychology*, 1977, 72(4), 775–790; Francis, D.H., and Sandberg, W.R. "Friendship Within Entrepreneurial Teams and Its Association with Team and Venture Performance," *Entrepreneurship: Theory and Practice*, 2000, 25(2), 5–15.

11. Rath, T. *Vital Friends: The People You Can't Afford to Live Without*. New York: Gallup Press, 2006, p. 52. See also Rath, T., and Harter, J. *Well Being: The Five Essential Elements*. New York: Gallup Press, 2010, pp. 40–43, for an update on this research.

12. Rath, T. *Vital Friends*.

13. Gabriel, A.S., Koopman, J., Rosen, C.C., Arnold, J.D., and Hochwarter, W.A. "Are Coworkers Getting in the Act? An Examination of Emotion Regulation in Coworker Exchanges," *Journal of Applied Psychology*, 2019, 105(8).

14. Nelson, B. *1001 Ways to Reward Employees* (2nd ed.). New York: Workman, 2005.

15. Carucci, R. "What Not to Do When You're Trying to Motivate Your Team," *Harvard Business Review*. Last modified July 16, 2018. Accessed at https://hbr.org/2018/07/what-not-to-do-when-youre-trying-to-motivate -your-team

16. Gibson, K.R., O'Leary, K., & Weintraub, J.R. "The Little Things That Make Employees Feel Appreciated," *Harvard Business Review*. Last modified January 23, 2020. Accessed at https://hbr.org/2020/01/the-little-things -that-make-employees-feel-appreciated

17. Martin and Marks, op. cit, p. 166.

18. Emmons, R.A. *Thanks! How Practicing Gratitude Makes You Happier*. New York: Houghton Mifflin, 2008. Also see Lesowitz, N. *Living Life as a Thank You: The Transformative Power of Daily Gratitude*. New York: Metro Books, 2009.

19. Brooks, D. *The Social Animal: The Hidden Sources of Love, Character, and Achievement*. New York: Random House, 2011.

20. Baker, W. *Achieving Success Through Social Capital: Tapping the Hidden Resources in Your Personal and Business Networks*. San Francisco: Jossey-Bass, 2000.

21. Geue, P.E. "Positive Practices in the Workplace: Impact on Team Climate, Work Engagement, and Task Performance," *The Journal of Applied Behavioral Science*, 2018, 54(3), 272–301.

22. Burkhart, B. "Getting New Employees Off to a Good Start," *New York Times*, March 13, 2013.

23. Parker, S. *The Village Effect: How Face-to-Face Contact Can Make Us Healthier and Happier*. New York: Penguin Random House, 2015.

24. Losada, M., and Heaphy, E. "The Role of Positivity and Connectivity in the Performance of Business Teams: A Nonlinear Dynamics Model," *American Behavioral Scientist,* 2004, 47(6), 740–765.

25. Berry, L.L., Parasuraman, A., and Zeithaml, V.A. "Improving Service Quality in America: Lessons Learned," *Academy of Management Executive,* 1994, 8(2), 32–45.

26. Stavrova, O., and Ehlebracht, D. "Cynical Beliefs About Human Nature and Income: Longitudinal and Cross-Cultural Analyses," *Journal of Personality and Social Psychology,* 110(1), 116–132.

27. Holt-Lunstad, J., Smith, T.B., Baker, M., Harris, T., and Stephenson, D. "Loneliness and Social Isolation as Risk Factors for Mortality: A Meta-Analytic Review," *Perspectives on Psychological Science,* March 2015, 10(2), 227–237.

28. McDowell, T., Ehteshami, S., and Sandell, K. "Are You Having Fun Yet?" *Deloitte Review,* 2019, (24).

29. Choi, Y.G., and Kwon, J. "Effects of Attitudes vs. Experience of Workplace Fun on Employee Behaviors," *International Journal of Contemporary Hospitality Management,* 2013, 25(1), 410–427; Georganta, K., and Montgomery, A. "Exploring Fun as a Job Resource: The Enhancing and Protecting Role of a Key Modern Workplace Factor," *International Journal of Applied Positive Psychology,* 2016, 1, 107–131.

30. Ford, R.C., McLaughlin, F.S., and Newstrom, J.W. "Questions and Answers About Fun at Work," *Human Resource Planning,* 2003, 26(4), 22.

31. Achor, S. *Happiness Advantage: The Seven Principles That Fuel Success and Performance at Work.* New York: Crown Business, 2010.

32. Gostick, A., and Christopher, S. *The Levity Effect: Why It Pays to Lighten Up.* Hoboken, NJ: Wiley, 2008.

33. Provine, R. *Laughter: A Scientific Investigation.* New York: Penguin, 2001.

34. Martin and Marks, op. cit.

35. Klein, G. *The Power of Intuition: How to Use Your Gut Feelings to Make Better Decisions at Work.* New York: Crown Business, 2004; Klein, G. *Streetlights and Shadows: Searching for the Keys to Adaptive Decision Making.* Boston: MIT Press, 2009.

Chapter 7: Leadership Is Self-Development

1. Kouzes, J.M., and Posner, B.Z. *LPI: Leadership Practices Inventory* (5th ed.). Hoboken, NJ: The Leadership Challenge–A Wiley Brand, 2017. https://www.leadershipchallenge.com/LeadershipChallenge/media/SiteFiles/resources/sample-reports/tlc-lpi-360-english-v5.pdf

Endnotes

2. Kouzes, J.M., and Posner, B.Z. *Learning Leadership: The Five Fundamentals of Becoming an Exemplary Leader*. San Francisco: The Leadership Challenge—A Wiley Brand, 2016.

3. Kouzes, T.K., and Posner, B.Z. "Influence of Managers' Mindset on Leadership Behavior," *Leadership & Organization Development Journal*, 2019, 53(8), 829–844. https://doi.org/10.1108/LODJ-03-3019-0142

4. Kolditz, T. "Why You Lead Determines How Well You Lead," *Harvard Business Review Blog*. Last modified July 22, 2014. https://hbr.org/2014/07/why-you-lead-determines-how-well-you-lead/ Accessed on April 5, 2020.

5. Duckworth, A. *Grit: The Power of Passion and Perseverance*. New York: Scribner, 2016.

6. Dutton, J.E. "Build High Quality Connections." In Dutton, J.E., and Spreitzer, G. (eds.), *How to Be a Positive Leader: Small Actions, Big Impact*. San Francisco, CA: Berrett-Koehler, 2014, pp. 11–21.

7. Whittaker, J. *A Life on the Edge: Memoirs of Everest and Beyond* (anniv. ed.). Seattle, WA: The Mountaineers, 2013, p. 16.

8. Brown, L.M., and Posner, B.Z. "Exploring the Relationship Between Learning and Leadership," *Leadership & Organization Development Journal*, May 2001, 274–280.

9. Bersin, J. "New Research Shows 'Heavy Learners' More Confident, Successful, and Happy at Work," LinkedIn. Last modified November 9, 2008. https://www.linkedin.com/pulse/want-happy-work-spend-time-learning-josh-bersin/ Accessed April 5, 2020.

10. Csikszentmihalyi, M. *Flow: The Psychology of Optimal Experience*. New York: Harper & Row, 1990.

ACKNOWLEDGMENTS

ONE OF THE undeniable truths about leading is *you can't do it alone.*
This is equally true about writing. One of the great joys of creating a
book is the opportunity to work with scores of talented, dedicated, and
inspiring people. We are profoundly grateful to all who've been on this
journey with us.

Foremost, we send our appreciation and admiration to the thousands of leaders without titles we've met over the years. You inspire us.
You are living proof that leadership is within every person who takes
the initiative to make something extraordinary happen, puts in the hard
work and dedication to make a difference, and remains open to learning
from the experiences. A very special thank you to all those leaders who
allowed us to share their stories and reflections. The lessons from your
experiences are the heartbeat of this book.

Another special shout-out of appreciation to Valarie Willis, who
originally urged us to write a book focusing on the amazing people who
make a difference without the benefit of title or position. Without Valarie's nudge, it's unlikely we would have started this project.

Working with us for over three decades of writing has been our uber
talented developmental editor, Leslie Stephen. As always, we are indebted

to her for generously and graciously applying her remarkable talents throughout the project. We also want to acknowledge our accomplished story editor, Nana Twumasi, for assisting us in developing many examples from the raw material into finished prose.

We are grateful to our colleagues at John Wiley & Sons, who have been constant supporters and loving critics. Jeanenne Ray, trade business editor, was the internal champion of this book. Her continuous coaching enabled us to produce a book that builds on the solid foundation of the past while creating a unique and distinctive volume for these times. Joining Jeanenne on the *Everyday People, Extraordinary Leadership* team were Michael Friedberg, marketing manager; Sally Baker, administrative support; Dawn Kilgore, managing editor; Shannon Vargo, publisher; Rebecca Taff, copy editor; Joanne Farness, proofreader; and Jayalakshmi Et, content specialist. We are blessed to be working with a passionate team of professionals who make us better every day.

We also give a standing ovation to Marisa Kelley, with whom we collaborated for two decades on The Leadership Challenge brand. Marisa was dedicated to giving our products the best life they could have and to building a community of coaches and facilitators to support the development of exemplary leaders around the globe. She always brings a ray of sunshine into every endeavor. Thanks also to Susan Rachmeler, Mark Scullard, Gabriel Sims, Alexandra Watson, and Kelly Wittnebel at Workplace Learning Solutions for their collaboration on a new designed learning experience that builds and enriches the capacity of emerging leaders.

As always, we cannot say enough about how appreciative we are of our immediate loved ones—to Tae and Nick, and to Jackie, Amanda, and Darryl, and to the next generation of leaders without titles, Rosalie and Julian. You bring great joy into our lives.

We wrote this book, as we have each of our books, in order to liberate the leader that lies within each person and to increase the quality and quantity of leaders for the world. Each and every individual matters. Each and every one makes a difference. The real challenge is to make sure that we're leaving the places we are a little bit better in the future as a result of our being there today. Let's be sure to live and lead life forward.

ABOUT THE AUTHORS

JIM KOUZES AND BARRY POSNER have been working together for nearly 40 years, studying leaders, researching leadership, conducting leadership development seminars, and providing leadership, with and without titles, in various capacities. They are coauthors of the award-winning, best-selling book *The Leadership Challenge*. Since its first edition in 1987, *The Leadership Challenge* has sold over 2.8 million copies worldwide and is available in more than 22 languages. It has won numerous awards, including the Critics' Choice Award from the nation's book review editors and book-of-the-year awards from both the American Council of Healthcare Executives and *Fast Company*. *The Leadership Challenge* is listed in *The Top 100 Business Books of All Time*, as one of the Top 10 books on leadership.

Jim and Barry have coauthored more than a dozen other award-winning leadership books, including *Leadership in Higher Education*; *Stop Selling & Start Leading*; *Learning Leadership: The Five Fundamentals for Becoming an Exemplary Leader*; *Turning Adversity into Opportunity*; *Finding the Courage to Lead*; *Great Leadership Creates Great Workplaces*; *Credibility: How Leaders Gain and Lose It, Why People Demand It*; *The Truth About Leadership: The No-Fads, Heart-of-the Matter Facts You*

Need to Know; *Encouraging the Heart: A Leader's Guide to Recognizing and Rewarding Others*; *A Leader's Legacy*; *Extraordinary Leadership in Australia and New Zealand*; *Making Extraordinary Things Happen in Asia*; and *The Student Leadership Challenge*.

Jim and Barry developed the widely used and highly acclaimed Leadership Practices Inventory (LPI), a 360-degree questionnaire assessing leadership behavior. The LPI has been completed by over five million people around the globe. Over 800 doctoral dissertations and academic research projects have been based on their The Five Practices of Exemplary Leadership framework. More information about their publications and research is available at www.leadershipchallenge.com. You can also sign up on the website for their monthly newsletter.

Among the honors and awards that Jim and Barry have received are the Association for Talent and Development's (ATD) highest award for their *Distinguished Contribution to Workplace Learning and Performance*; named Management/Leadership Educators of the Year by the International Management Council; ranked by *Leadership Excellence* magazine in the top 20 on their list of the Top 100 Thought Leaders; named by *Coaching for Leadership* in the Top 50 Leadership Coaches in the nation; considered by *HR Magazine* as one of the Most Influential International Thinkers; and listed among the Top 75 Management Experts in the World by *Inc.* magazine.

Jim and Barry are frequent keynote speakers, and each has conducted leadership development programs for hundreds of organizations, including Apple, Applied Materials, ARCO, AT&T, Australia Institute of Management, Australia Post, Bank of America, Bose, Charles Schwab, Cisco Systems, Clorox, Community Leadership Association, Conference Board of Canada, Consumers Energy, Deloitte Touche, Dow Chemical, Egon Zehnder International, Federal Express, Genentech, Google, Gymboree, HP, IBM, Intel, Itau Unibanco, Jobs DR-Singapore, Johnson & Johnson, Kaiser Foundation Health Plans and Hospitals, L.L. Bean, Lawrence Livermore National Labs, Lucile Packard Children's Hospital, Merck, Motorola, NetApp, Northrop Grumman, Novartis, Oakwood Housing, Oracle, Petronas, Roche Bioscience, Siemens, 3M, Toyota, the U.S. Postal Service, United Way, USAA, Verizon, VISA, Westpac, and

The Walt Disney Company. In addition, they have presented seminars and lectures at over 100 college and university campuses.

Jim Kouzes is a fellow at the Doerr Institute for New Leaders at Rice University and has been the Dean's Executive Fellow of Leadership, Leavey School of Business, at Santa Clara University. He lectures on leadership around the world to corporations, governments, and nonprofits. He is a highly regarded leadership scholar, an experienced executive, and the *Wall Street Journal* cited him as one of the 12 best executive educators in the United States. Jim has received the Thought Leadership Award from the Instructional Systems Association, the most prestigious award given by the trade association of training and development industry providers, and the Golden Gavel, the highest honor awarded by Toastmasters International.

Jim served as president, CEO, and chairman of the Tom Peters Company for 11 years, and led the Executive Development Center at Santa Clara University for seven years. He was the founder and executive director for eight years of the Joint Center for Human Services Development at San Jose State University and was on the staff of the School of Social Work, University of Texas. His career in training and development began in 1969 when he conducted seminars for Community Action Agency staff and volunteers in the war on poverty. Following graduation from Michigan State University (B.A. degree with honors in political science), he served as a Peace Corps volunteer (1967–1969). You can reach Jim directly at jim@kouzes.com.

Barry Posner holds the Michael J. Accolti, S.J. Chair at Santa Clara University and is Professor of Leadership with the Leavey School of Business and chair of the Department of Management and Entrepreneurship. He previously served for six years as Associate Dean for Graduate Education, six years as Associate Dean for Executive Education, and 12 years as Dean of the School. He has been a distinguished visiting professor around the globe: Hong Kong University of Science and Technology, Sabanci University (Istanbul), University of Western Australia, and University of Auckland. At Santa Clara he has received the President's Distinguished Faculty Award, the School's Extraordinary Faculty Award, and several other outstanding teaching and academic honors. An internationally renowned scholar and educator, Barry is author or coauthor of more than 100 research and practitioner-focused articles. He currently serves on the editorial boards for *Leadership and Organizational Development Journal* and *The International Journal of Servant-Leadership*, and is a recipient of the *Journal of Management Inquiry*'s Outstanding Scholar Award for Career Achievement.

Barry received his baccalaureate degree with honors in political science from the University of California, Santa Barbara, his master's degree in public administration from The Ohio State University, and his doctoral degree in organizational behavior and administrative theory from the University of Massachusetts, Amherst. Having consulted worldwide with many public and private sector organizations, he also works at a strategic level with a number of community-based and professional organizations, currently sitting on the board of directors of SVCreates. He has served previously on the board of the American Institute of Architects (AIA), Big Brothers/Big Sisters of Santa Clara County, Center for Excellence in Nonprofits, Junior Achievement of Silicon Valley and Monterey Bay, Public Allies, San Jose Repertory Theater, Sigma Phi Epsilon Fraternity, Uplift Family Services, and several start-up companies. Barry can be reached directly at bposner@scu.edu.

INDEX

Index

We know you have what it takes to lead.

The Leadership Challenge® is the gold standard in leadership development. For 35+ years we have helped millions unlock their leadership potential by providing the tools—including the LPI®: Leadership Practices Inventory®—and training to model the way, inspire a shared vision, challenge the process, enable others to act, and encourage others. Together we can unlock your inner leader.

Visit our website to start your leadership journey
leadershipchallenge.com/EPEL

More from the Authors

The LPI®

The Leadership Challenge Training

More From the Authors

James M. Kouzes and Barry Z. Posner are the coauthors of the international bestselling books *The Leadership Challenge, The Truth About Leadership, A Leader's Legacy, Encouraging the Heart*, and more than a dozen other books and workbooks on leadership. Their work continues to instruct, inspire, and model the way for emerging and experienced leaders across the world.

For more information, please visit

Leadershipchallenge.com/EPEL